Finding
Karen

Finding Karen

An Ancestral Mystery

Dorothy Allred Solomon

TEXAS TECH UNIVERSITY PRESS

This book is typeset in Cardo. The paper used in this book meets the min-
imum requirements of ANSI/NISO Z39.48-1992 (R1997). ∞

Designed by Hannah Gaskamp
Cover design by Hannah Gaskamp

Library of Congress Cataloging-in-Publication Data

Names: Solomon, Dorothy Allred, author.
Title: Finding Karen: An ancestral mystery / Dorothy Allred Solomon.
Description: Lubbock, Texas: Texas Tech University Press, [2020] | Series:
Judith Keeling books | Includes bibliographical references and index. |
Summary: "Account of the author's Danish great-great-grandmother,
who converted to Mormonism, emigrated to the United States in the
mid-nineteenth century, and struggled with life in the new country and,
like the author herself, the concept of plural marriage."—Provided by
publisher.
Identifiers: LCCN 2020008272 (print) | LCCN 2020008273 (ebook) |
ISBN 9781682830611 (paperback; alk. paper) | ISBN 9781682830628 (ebook)
Subjects: LCSH: Sorensen, Karen, 1832–1908. | Mormons—Utah—
Biography. | Church of Jesus Christ of Latter-Day Saints—Biography.
Classification: LCC BX8695.S758 S65 2020 (print) | LCC BX8695.S758
(ebook) | DDC 289.3092 [B]—dc23
LC record available at https://lccn.loc.gov/2020008272
LC ebook record available at https://lccn.loc.gov/2020008273

Printed in the United States of America
20 21 22 23 24 25 26 27 28 / 9 8 7 6 5 4 3 2 1

Texas Tech University Press
Box 41037
Lubbock, Texas 79409-1037 USA
800.832.4042
ttup@ttu.edu
www.ttupress.org

This book is dedicated to two pillars of my universe: my husband, Bruce C. Solomon, and my editor, Judith Keeling. It is also dedicated to Karen Sorensen Rasmussen, who exercised the courage to live her convictions, and to my children and grandchildren, living proof that in knowing our past we can sculpt a better future.

Contents

A Brief Chronology

Situating Karen's Story within the History of The Church of Jesus Christ of Latter-day Saints

[Note: Like Karen, Allred family members are author's ancestors]

- December 23, 1805: Joseph Smith Jr. is born to Lucy Mack and Joseph Smith Sr., Sharon, Vermont.

- Spring 1820: Joseph Smith has his First Vision of God, the Father, and His Son, Jesus Christ.

- September 21–22, 1823: Joseph Smith is visited by the Angel Moroni, who tells of the history of an ancient people. He reveals gold plates hidden in the nearby Hill Cumorah, which will become the *Book of Mormon*.

- September 22, 1823: Joseph Smith retrieves the plates, intending to translate their ancient script into English.

- January 17, 1827: Joseph Smith and Emma Hale elope and marry in New York.

- June 1829: The translation of the gold plates is complete.

- March 26, 1830: First copies of the *Book of Mormon* are printed.

- April 6, 1830: The church to be called The Church of Jesus Christ of Latter-day Saints is organized near Fayette, New York.

- December 1830: The Latter-day Saints begin to gather in Ohio. Eliza R. Snow meets Joseph Smith in the home of her parents near Mantua.

- July 1831: Latter-day Saints are redirected to Independence,

Missouri. Great-great-great-grandmother Mary Calvert Allred is baptized.

- April 3, 1832: Karen Sorensen (Sorensdatter) is born to Ane Magrette Baltzarsen (Baltzarsdatter) and Soren Pedersen in Bjergene, Holme, Aarhus, Denmark.

- November 7, 1833: Saints flee Jackson County, Missouri, driven by mobs to Clay County, Missouri, and from there to Caldwell County. Twenty Allred families are caught in this forced emigration.

- May–June 1834: Joseph Smith leads "Zion's Camp" from Ohio to bring relief for the Missouri Saints. Great-great-great grandfather Isaac Allred is baptized.

- October 1838: In the Latter-day Saints settlement of Far West, Missouri, Joseph Smith and his brethren are charged with treason and condemned by General Samuel D. Lucas to immediate execution, which is averted by General Doniphan who refused to commit murder. Mormon Militia (including Great-great grandfather William Moore Allred) and other Latter-day Saints are under siege and must surrender weapons and property before being driven out. They emigrate to Nauvoo, Illinois.

- December 1, 1838: Joseph Smith and others are imprisoned in the Liberty Jail in Missouri. En route to a hearing, Joseph and his brethren are allowed to escape on April 15, 1839.

- April 22, 1839: Joseph Smith arrives in Illinois.

- March 17, 1842: Relief Society, the women's auxiliary of the Church, is organized in Nauvoo, Illinois.

- June 29, 1842: Eliza Roxcy Snow marries Joseph Smith, becoming his fourteenth or fifteenth plural wife.

- June 27, 1844: While awaiting trial in the Carthage Jail in Illinois for treason and inciting riot after destroying the defamatory *Nauvoo Expositor*, the Prophet Joseph Smith and his brother, Church Patriarch Hyrum Smith, are assassinated by an armed mob of 200.

- August 8, 1844: Brigham Young is sustained to the leadership of the Church.

- March 1845: Brigham Young suspends the Relief Society.

- July 1846–July 1847: Under pressure from the United States government, approxmiately 500 Latter-day Saint men join the Mormon Battalion, including Isaac's twin sons Reddin and Reddick Allred.

- April 1847: President Brigham Young leads his pioneer company from Winter Quarters, Nebraska, to journey across the Great Plains and the Rocky Mountains.

- July 24, 1847: Desperately sick, Brigham Young raises his head to see the Salt Lake Valley from Emigration Point and declares, "This is the right place."

- May–June 1849: Crickets devastate the badly needed Latter-day Saint crops.

- May 25, 1849: The Constitutional Act of Denmark is ratified, promising freedom of religion and education for all Danes, male or female.

- October 10, 1849: Great-great-great-grandfather Isaac Allred arrives in the Salt Lake Valley.

- July 1851: The first translation of the *Book of Mormon* from English to another language, Danish, becomes available to converts in Scandinavia.

- August 28, 1852: Church Historian Orson Hyde publicly announces that The Church of Jesus Christ of Latter-day Saints endorses and practices plural marriage.

- October 9, 1854: Karen Sorensen converts to The Church of Jesus Christ of Latter-day Saints and is baptized in Denmark.

- March 27, 1857: Mads Peder Rasmussen converts to The Church of Jesus Christ of Latter-day Saints and is baptized in Denmark.

- October–November 1856: The Willie and Martin Handcart Companies, which left late in August, are caught in early winter snows. Tragedy results, with a combined total of 213 of 980 losing their lives and many others losing appendages to frostbite.

- May 1857–July 1858: In the Utah War (also known as the Utah Expedition, Buchanan's Blunder, and the Mormon Rebellion), an estimated one hundred fifty lives are lost, including the 120 migrants killed in the Mountain Meadows massacre of Southern Utah in September and six Californians murdered in the Aiken massacre in October 1857.

- 1857: The Perpetual Emigration Fund is suspended because of the Utah War, economic woes in Europe, and reports of the Willie and Martin Handcart disaster. Many converts in England and Scandinavia, including Karen, must postpone their plans for emigration.

- April 1, 1859: The *L.N. Hvidt* carries Karen Sorensen and other Scandinavian converts over the tempestuous North Sea to Grimsby, England.

- April 3, 1859: Karen Sorensen turns twenty-seven years old aboard ship.

- April 11, 1859: Karen Sorensen and Mads Peder Rasmussen join 725 Latter-day Saint emigrants on the *William Tapscott* leaving Liverpool, England.

- April 11–May 1, 1859: Sometime during this window, Karen and Mads are married aboard the *William Tapscott*, with the union solemnized by the head of the 1859 immigration company, President Robert F. Neslen.

- May 14, 1859: The *William Tapscott* arrives at Castle Garden, New York.

- June 7, 1859: The George Rowley Handcart Company leaves Florence, Nebraska, with a total of 235 saints.

- June 23, 1859: The Robert F. Neslen Company departs Florence with 380 souls.

- September 15, 1859: Mads and Karen arrive in Salt Lake City.

- Spring 1860: Mads and Karen settle in Centerville, Utah.

- May 16, 1860: Mads and Karen are sealed for eternity in the Salt Lake Endowment House.

- April 1860: Laura Rasmussen is born to Karen and Mads in Centerville.

- November 1860: Baby Laura dies in Centerville.

- August 1862: Peter Rasmussen is born to Karen and Mads in Centerville.

- Spring 1863: The Rasmussens move to Richville in Morgan County, Utah.

- Summer 1863: Ane Magrette Baltzarsdatter and Soren Pedersen emigrate to Richville, Utah, on the *B.S. Kimball*.

- July 13, 1864: Mary Catrena Rasmussen is born to Mads and Karen in Richville.

- Summer 1866: The Rasmussens move to Farmington, Utah.

- September 8, 1866: George Henry Rasmussen is born to Karen and Mads in Farmington.

- Late December 1866: Brigham Young calls Eliza R. Snow to work with bishops to organize the Relief Society and later to instruct the sisters, making her essentially the de facto president of the Relief Society. The title was not formalized until 1880 by third Church president John Taylor.

- 1869: Karen returns to her paternal family in Richville.

- 1869: Karen gives birth to twins, Annie Margret and Joseph Soren.

- December 1869: The Cullom Bill, meant to reinforce the Morrill Anti-Bigamy Act of 1862, is introduced.

- January 13, 1870: The Great Indignation Meeting in the Salt Lake Tabernacle is held to protest the Cullom Bill and allow Latter-day Saint women to express their views on polygamy and female franchise. Between five and six thousand women attend.

- February 12, 1870: Acting Governor of Utah Territory S. A. Mann signs a bill granting women suffrage.

- February 14, 1870: Twenty-six female residents of Utah Territory, enfranchised two days earlier by the Utah Legislature, comprise the first group of women in the United States to legally exercise their right to vote. (Wyoming Territory women were previously granted suffrage but had yet to exercise their right.)

- April 1872: Peter Rasmussen, son of Karen and Mads, drowns in a swollen river near Bear Lake, Utah.

- July 24, 1887: (Forty years to the day after the first pioneers entered the Salt Lake Valley) Mads Peder Rasmussen dies in Vernal, Uintah County, Utah.

- July 10, 1908: Karen Sorensen [Rasmussen Cheney] dies in Morgan, Weber County, Utah.

Preface: Why

A PERSON CAN LIVE with contradictory elements for only so long before seeking to integrate them. I am an example of that urge: Raised in Mormon fundamentalism, the twenty-eighth of my father's forty-eight children and born to his fourth plural wife, I chose to marry monogamously. Throughout my life I've wondered why a committed individualist was born into a family so fused to religion and ever ready to surrender selfhood.

This quest for understanding generated my first book, *In My Father's House* — the first contemporary memoir of polygamy — and two that followed. It's hardly surprising that an essentially middle child among so many would one day choose to have a small family and a husband all to herself. More surprising have been the dilemmas that choice would entail. One may marry monogamously, but one doesn't cease to be the product of polygamy. The imprint of family isn't something to be shed like a snakeskin — nor could I want to shed the bonds of love I knew growing up. However, I weighed the problems of that life against my personal convictions and found that I could not maintain integrity and live as my parents had. While I keep faith with many of the spiritual principles of my upbringing, I do so in my own fashion. I find myself perpetually struggling, as Fitzgerald suggested, to hold in mind two opposing ideas without losing the ability to function. I try to practice the art of amalgamation — to reconcile what I cherish in my big fundamentalist family with the person I've become and must be. Rather than throwing out the baby of faith with the bathwater of circumspection, I'm learning how to hold onto what works and let go of what won't. Yet the more I seek to sort out what can and can't be left behind, the more the complexities of my history seek me out, carrying lessons I don't always want to learn — and in the case of this work, some for which I'm immensely grateful.

As I've sought to integrate dissonant aspects of my being, I've been particularly haunted by issues pertaining to gender roles. How, I've wondered, can I emulate ancestors who sacrificed homeland and family for a new world and a new way of being — an entirely admirable feat — when I cannot reconcile their complicity in compromising their daughters' wholeness? How is it that my sisterhood, the women of Mormonism, made up the first group of American women to cast their votes in a general election, yet a century later voted overwhelmingly against the Equal Rights Amendment? How can true faith hold to such a spirit-crushing double standard? Moreover, could I be contained by a doctrine that offered treasures such as eternal family and modern miracles without safeguarding the dignity and value of women? Such contradictions in the culture that spawned me are no less complicated than those I see in myself, creating a chasm too wide to cross through pure logic. Because I could not otherwise see my future on the other side, I have sought to resolve the dissonance by delving into the past.

I have trust issues with myself: I am sometimes blindered by self-righteousness that has manifested in rebelliousness. As a teenager, I would engage in standoffs with my father, one so heated that he slapped my face and call me a hussy. Only later did I understand the true nature of our disagreement, which was more about the sting of disrespect we both felt than anything else. He saw himself protecting me, and I saw myself claiming agency, thinking for myself. So intractable were we in our separate versions of right that this habitually gentle man could see no other way to reach across the divide. In the end, I didn't run away from home, and my father agreed that I would skip Sunday meetings with the fundamentalist group. Today, I'm still not sure what was most important to me at the time — that I get my way or that I prove my father wrong. Over the years, my need to be right has abated, but my system still revels in the dose of dopamine released each time I'm convinced I've been vindicated — especially if some adversary is displaced in the process. This self-righteousness demands scrutiny and requires transformation because the dynamic of be-right and make-wrong destroys friendships, catalyzes divorces, and starts wars. Life repeatedly teaches me that an overweening insistence on a singular version of reality eclipses relationships as well as a larger, clearer view of history. This book has become a testament to the difference between fitting evidence to a cherished conviction and objectively seeking truth.

When I started this project, I had crossed what I considered the cusp of mid-life. My husband and I were empty nesters. Sometimes we looked across the table and saw a stranger sitting there. Little irritants and big disagreements generated a persistent tension that reminded me of earlier years when the man I had married waxed and waned with the tides of PTSD. I felt I could survive in my marriage only by finding ballast, whatever that might be, within myself.

Each day I faced the pressure of my diminishing years of productivity. I reflected on my life works and wondered what difference I had truly made, if only in the eyes and lives of my children and grandchildren. I contemplated the growing schism I felt as over the years I took exception — in print as well as in my heart — to my native culture's stance on gender roles.

It was time, I decided, to deepen my understanding of gender issues in Latter-day Saint history. I browsed through forgotten listings in rare book collections and dusted the worn bindings of journals, ferreting through personal libraries and paging through buried, out-of-print testimonials. The more I read, the more I marveled at the strength of pioneer women. I was delighted by their pride, initiative, and self-possession; I longed for the congruity of their faith, the security of their inclusion. I wanted to feel such power and belonging; I wanted to be true to myself and yet to belong to the community. These pioneers seemed very assertive compared to the women I had known in the fundamentalist group of my childhood. They also seemed different from most of the women I had known in The Church of Jesus Christ, with cherished exceptions.

For Latter-day Saints, handcart pioneers epitomize the essence of unwavering faith and perseverance, the sort of strength and constancy that my father always pointed to in his great-grandmother Karen. He told us that Karen had left her native Denmark, sailed the stormy Atlantic, then pulled a handcart across the Great Plains and the Rocky Mountains to congregate with other saints in Mormon Zion, in the Salt Lake Valley of Utah. When my father wanted to pose a female example of familial loyalty and religious devotion, he spoke of this handcart grandmother, praising her perseverance despite poverty, persecution, and other adversity. I remember sitting on the living room rug amid thirty or so brothers and sisters, the back of my neck tingling as I imagined facing a line of hostile Sioux on the Great Plains or pulling a heavy handcart up a mountain while being stalked by wolves. I wondered how I deserved to be in the bloodline of such a brave woman, especially since I craved my warm bath and soft bed more than most.

As an adult, I had to speculate why in comparison to Karen and my other grandmothers, I seemed to lack devotion, both familial and religious. Had I not turned away from my family's faith and for a time tried on one religion after another like a woman shopping for an overcoat? Had I not, when faced with continuous poverty and persecution, fled my outlaw family? Had I not published family secrets, such betrayal seeming the opposite of loyalty? I would look in the mirror at my haunted green eyes and wonder what I had missed along the way.

Through my grandmothers, I descend from sword-wives who fought alongside their men, from farmers who forced unforgiving terrain to yield crops, from Nordics who survived intemperate weather and tempestuous neighbors. My Scandinavian grandmothers shared the Valkyries' ability to swoop in, encompass the dissent of warriors and the wanderlust of sailors, and carry their men back to the hearth or away to Valhalla. Shouldn't their exuberant Viking genes and powerful ambitions be mine too, welcoming a raised ceiling of consciousness and throwing open panoramas of possibility? Shouldn't I have inherited the stamina to contain dissent without losing my family or any part of myself? Might knowing them offer a rubric that could grant me the balance and stability I needed now?

Compelled by these questions, I drove one morning in February 2012 from my home amid the multicolored mesas of sunny St. George, Utah, to overcast and frigid Salt Lake City. I made my way through slushy downtown traffic and clusters of homeless people outside the Utah History Research Center housed in the old Rio Grande Depot. The depot is a marvel of Renaissance Revival architecture, designed by renowned architect of churches Henry Schlacks, who endowed it with vaulted ceilings, high-arched windows, and Yule marble columns. I stood before the enormous double doors and wondered if anything of my grandmothers lay sequestered among the historical remnants housed in this beautiful old building. I hoped that some scrap of memory or fact might illuminate my struggles as I passed from the frozen air into a gust of heat. As I gazed upward, the apex sucked me into a time warp that would hold me for many months.

In the oak-paneled library, I found the life story of my father's maternal grandfather, my great-grandfather Arthur Benjamin Clark, thus opening the door to his daughter, my grandmother Evelyn, and to his wife, my great-grandmother Mary Catrena, and through her, to his mother-in-law, my great-great-grandmother Karen — the handcart pioneer of my father's stories.

Arthur B. Clark was a fiddle player and an itinerant dentist who set the family standard of making house calls to people in pain, a pattern Mary Catrena sustained, as did my father, calling at the homes of those who were birthing or broken or dying throughout the west. Inside the drafty splendor of the Rio Grande Depot, I pored over a fat volume bound in brown leather patinaed with the oils of hands I had never touched, relatives long dead. My own fingers stiff with cold, I scratched notes on a yellow legal pad, breathing the dust and mildew of biographical pages as I followed Arthur's travels through the mountain glens of Idaho, where he'd been sent by Church authorities to practice polygamy. He moved into the Star Valley of Wyoming, where politics focused on cattle barons and homesteaders instead of rounding up polygamists, and helped to settle the town of Freedom, Wyoming. In 1890, he slipped across the border into Utah with Pinkerton detectives on his tail and traveled to the Salt Lake Tabernacle to hear the manifesto outlawing polygamy read at The Church of Jesus Christ's General Conference by President Wilford Woodruff. Afterward, upon the advice of his church leaders, Arthur took a train that may have passed through this very depot on his way to Colorado and from there to the red dust of Chihuahua, Mexico, so that he could maintain relationship with his five plural wives, Great-grandmother Mary Catrena among them.

Mary Catrena's history, subsumed into Arthur's, was spare, yet it contained detail about her own mother that changed everything for me: In 1854, Karen had been cast out of the Danish Lutheran home headed by her father, Soren Pedersen, because she joined The Church of Jesus Christ of Latter-day Saints. Her father reacted to the prospect of her entering a potentially polygamous way of life with the indignation my father had shown at the prospect of any of his children abandoning it. I remembered the raised voices, the accusations, the implied threat: You are my child; believe as I believe or leave. Had my father known about his great-grandmother's trial of faith? And if so . . . . The binder holding those fragile pages slipped from my hands and thudded shut against the oak table, startling other patrons who shot irritated glances my way. Flushed with discovery and embarrassment, I ducked my head and reopened the biography, delicately turning to Mary Catrena's history again. There I found the name of the packet ship on which Karen sailed, the year of her departure from Copenhagen, and the date of her arrival in the United States. Included was a blurred copy of a ship's manifest penned before the *William Tapscott* sailed from Liverpool; it had been signed by the agent, a regional missionary leader named Asa Calkin. On the manifest I read *Karen Sorensen, age 27.* The age and name fit neatly with the ancestral pages of my own book of remembrance, put together as a seminary project during my teenage years.

Other details proved harder to find that day — and were less stunning — but after taking copious notes on the Clark biography, I left the Rio Grande terminal under its spell and knew I had to press on. Outside, a bitter wind blowing across the Great Salt Lake stirred a skiff of snow sheeting the parking lot. The burgeoning huddle of homeless people smoked and murmured, rubbing their hands and stomping their feet, waiting for the mission up the street to open and feed them supper. As I scraped ice off the windshield of my car, I thought of Karen, homeless in the Denmark winter, and wondered where she had sheltered after her father threw her out of the house that night, preceding roughly five years of homelessness and persecution before she found the means to emigrate.

Back home in the sunshine of St. George, I tried to refocus on the original project of ferreting out gender patterns in Mormon culture, but Karen haunted me. I thought about her insistence on doing what she felt was right despite her father's objections. I, too, had followed my conscience, much to my father's dismay. Could the ancestor whose pristine character put me to shame be the ancestor with whom I had the most in common? I launched into immigrant histories and read about typical Danish housing and diet, about the prevailing political and religious attitudes of 1850s Danes, about ridicule and castigation of Latter-day Saints, about the interventions conducted with converts, and the kidnapping of LDS missionaries. I unearthed information I'd gathered from Rhea Kunz, my father's half-sister by Grandfather Harvey Allred's first wife. The notes I had taken when interviewing Aunt Rhea after my father's death were corroborated in her writings, *Voices of Women: Approbating Celestial or Plural Marriage.* Aunt Rhea wrote that Karen had pulled a handcart, that she had just turned twenty-seven years old when she emigrated, and that her name was Karen Sorensen. When I correlated the entry on a ship's masthead with her name on the George Rowley handcart company roster, I concluded that I had found my handcart grandmother. With this discovery cached in my heart, I read and wrote voraciously for more than a year. I devoured the history of Karen's time, the busiest immigration era. I diligently tracked the first women's movement in the United States and held up a feminist lens to view Karen's life.

As tunnel visioned as my pursuit of her seems, I could see Karen's story at the center of a broader canvas, a particular study of gender and agency revealed in the trials borne by strong women in a pioneering, patriarchal culture. I had a skeletal version of her life's journey, but I needed to see her struggling with the roles expected of her and enduring the experiences that forged her character. Lacking a diary or journal in Karen's hand, I began reading the records of others who made the crossing with Karen, losing entire afternoons as I devoured whole journals in a single sitting. Details specific to Karen were harder to come by. I realized I would have to reach out — probably beyond my comfort zone — to ferret out information from family members I scarcely knew and, as it would turn out, beyond my paternal family. That knowledge sent me scurrying back to what was sure, the family record cobbled together when my parents were living and I was young.

The white cardboard cover of my own Book of Remembrance is dog-eared, and the pages have begun to yellow, testament to my own declining arc. A fading line juts from the photo of myself to my father and from there to Grandmother Evelyn. Diagonal lines connect her to Great-grandmother Mary Catrena and a fuzzy portrait of a middle-aged woman above a smudged name and birthdate: Karen Sorensen, April 3, 1832. Her hair shines in the platinum corona of my Danish line and her eyes have the almond cast of some Scandinavian tribes; Karen looks beyond the camera, wearing an expression meant to be serene but betrayed by the downward curve of her mouth. Her expression illuminated contradictions I'd seen in myself. Would Karen's example help me to outstrip disappointments, betrayals, and regrets? Would her life help me to understand the beautiful but sometimes brutal dance between men and women, between parents and children? Could she teach me the crucial strategies of love and forgiveness?

Given that Latter-day Saints are avidly record-keeping people, it was surprising that so little information about her was available.

Thus, I'm grateful for every narrative that includes her, gathered from the memories and memoirs preserved by relatives and various ancestral sites. In piecing together her story I've had to rely on scraps—a set of immigrant records and a handful of journals not her own: the history of her husband as told by three of his daughters, the life stories of her second son and her grandsons. I have sought her name in the diaries and autobiographies of my father and grandfather. I found women's perspectives on Karen's life in the account of my father's half-sister by another mother and in the stories told by my own mother, neither of them Karen's blood relatives.

Many unanswered questions remain about why her history has not been formally written, given the breadth and peculiarity of her life. The first regards her capability: Could she have written her own life story? She was educated in Denmark's public school and she learned English eagerly. Why, then, did Karen leave no personal story? Did she believe her life so mundane and inconsequential that it wasn't worth recording? Had parents or husband convinced her that the thoughts, feelings, and experiences of a woman couldn't matter, or that it was somehow shameful for a woman to make history? I doubt this, for there is evidence that she was neither meek nor accommodating, but impatient and headstrong. The challenges of immigration testify that she wasn't low on courage. Well, then, was her faith fragile or crumbling, leaving her tongue-tied as sometimes I have been? I think not. Her initial courage in leaving her father's house never wavered; she never abandoned her decision to join The Church of Jesus Christ of Latter-day Saints even though she encountered enormous disappointments during her membership. Was she so engaged in sheer survival that she couldn't spare the energy to write? As I think of my exuberant father and his siblings, I doubt that the quotidian kept her from picking up a pen and putting it to paper. Well, then, did regret and disappointment snip the threads of her tale? This is possible, even probable. Perhaps, as would Martha Hughes Cannon—pioneer physician, first female state senator, and fifth plural wife—Karen destroyed her own journals to keep future eyes from judging her secrets and mistakes and to protect others. But given that we are all secret-keepers and sinners and that we inadvertently complicate the lives of those we love, her very humanness argues against leaving her name blank or unadorned.

In researching Karen, I have become acquainted with other ancestors as well: Karen's mother, Ane Magrette Baltzarsdatter, and her father, Soren Pedersen (also known as Soren Dalsgaard because as a young man he worked as an apprentice on the farm of Andres Dals) had to survive their own dichotomies. Ane was refined and educated, from a well-to-do family; Soren was born a peasant with little more to offer than his heart and the work of his hands. I've even come to know Karen's husband, my ephemeral great-great-grand-father Mads Peder Rasmussen. My father never spoke of him, nor did my grandmother speak of her grandfather. Mads was the blank oval on the family tree, the ghost in the basement, the stuff of fantasies and nightmares. While seeking Karen in immigration records and ships' manifests and in the pages of diaries and history books, I repeatedly encountered the elusive Mads as well.

In some avenues of Mormondom, there's a notion that one's ancestors, along with the spirits of family yet to be born, act as one's guardian angels. In my early twenties, as I began writing, I experienced the muse-like influence of departed family. I would get stuck on a half-written page, casting about for facts and details that didn't seem to exist. Then I'd meet someone in my dreams who pointed a direction or told a story, someone who looked like one of my parents or grandparents.

I come from a family that puts stock in dreams. That is, marriages have been made and lives altered by dreams. In my first book, I told the story of my grandfather Harvey meeting his second and plural wife, Grandmother Evelyn, in a dream before he encountered her, on the steps of the chapel in Afton, Wyoming. When I was in my late twenties, a few months before my father was murdered in his office by the thirteenth wife of Ervil LeBaron, my departed Grandmother Evelyn visited me in a dream. She showed me a jar of spoiled fruit and opened it; a black widow spider jumped out. The dream moved me to go to my father, despite our estrangement, to tell him that I feared for his safety. The visit yielded a healing conversation wherein to my great surprise he encouraged my writing (nonfiction! he urged). Whatever else one can dismiss about dreams, without this one we would have missed our chance to reconcile. Even now I flinch to think how much more painful my grief would have been.

In addition to dreams about those grandparents who knew me and held me, I have had dreams about others I never met in this life. I may have encountered Karen in one of those dreams. In researching and writing this book, I felt as though I'd met her long ago. Often, I sensed that I wasn't always the one holding the lantern as I explored the caves of family history and the recesses of my own soul.

I can claim intrinsic knowledge of Karen through the resonance of genetic memory. She speaks to me through the intelligence of the body, lessons passed to me that I don't realize until I'm faced with situations that demand an immediate and specific response. I have a sense of the impatient energy she bestowed on her granddaughter, my grandmother Evelyn, a tall long-legged woman with elbows as sharp as her Danish cheekbones, and silvery-blonde hair like Karen's. Evelyn also had Karen's tall brow and intent blue eyes, passed on to my father and all four of my children. She was an intense, edgy woman who always seemed to be herding the people around her. In her later years, my father brought her to live on our family compound in a little log cabin adjoining the house where I was born. She would bang on my mother's bedroom window with her cane until someone came to do her bidding. Evelyn was the grandmother who told me I was different from other children and that I must learn to take care of myself. She warned me not to hold babies responsible for my happiness — they would grow up and do whatever they wanted, she said, and I might not like what they chose. I learned from Grandmother Evelyn that women could be strong in the face of life's disappointments and tragedies. Her very presence spoke of the steep prices and ample rewards of being a woman, of being married, of being alive. I know she learned these lessons on her own, but she had also inherited an inclination toward sacrifice and strength and, like any mother, passed it on to her progeny.

Evelyn's mother, Mary Catrena, died before I was born. Although her life didn't span oceans and religions as did Karen's, significant traces of Mary Catrena have shown up in my siblings and myself and in my children and grandchildren. A pioneer of Idaho and Wyoming, she was nurse and midwife to Shoshone and Ute, and later to Mexican neighbors as well as to her own people. My father became a doctor and delivered some six thousand babies in his lifetime. My eldest daughter, Denise, is a labor-and-delivery nurse who coaches women of every race and nationality through the rigors of giving birth; she has Mary Catrena's eyes and her gift for healing. Mary Catrena navigated overweening patriarchy, forced emigration, and mandatory polygamy and kept her identity intact while serving her fellow beings. I wonder what she thought of her mother, if she struggled in their relationship, and why she didn't record more about

Karen. Karen, who rebelled against the status quo, who disregarded her father's dictates, who struck out on her own without familial footsteps to follow. Karen, whose unwavering faith—in self, in life, and in God—might bolster my own. Karen, whose journey could validate my own.

From my first visit to the Rio Grande Depot's historical library I knew that Karen deserved to have her story recovered, whatever its truths. But distilling truth has not been easy for me: As a child I learned to fabricate lies for my family's protection at roughly the same time I learned to speak. In adulthood, I have tried to school myself in the elements of honesty. I have sifted through the stories of my forebears, asking what is real. And now, counting on the true north of my handcart grandmother, I am committed to piecing together Karen's life.

Karen was the first in her family to join an American-born religion and immigrate to the new world. She was part of that great wave of western migration, the gathering of those who were building a promised land in America. What follows combines two journeys: Karen's and my own as I came to know her better. I hope that I've illuminated Karen's steadfast courage and her immutable autonomy. I hope I've shown the driving force of her faith in God and in personal agency. Daughters and granddaughters in my native culture tend to set down their dreams to take up family burdens, then often forget to pick up their own lives again. Sons and grandsons also sacrifice bits of themselves to the religious culture, suffering a thousand cuts as they strive for righteous manhood. May these daughters and sons learn from Karen as I have—and from my own prideful missteps along the way to finding her.

Finding Karen

CHAPTER I

Come to Zion

I SET KAREN APART from a string of remarkable ancestors because she exercised her agency even though her early life was rooted in the strictest of Danish Lutheran households. This fusion of will and devotion may be why, at twenty-two years old, Karen still lived with her parents in a state perilously close to spinsterhood by the standard of the day. She was the first of six children, including a younger sister who died in childhood. As the eldest, the industrious Karen was probably much appreciated by her mother, a well-bred lady without the means to hire servants.

The cultured Ane Magrette Baltzarsdatter had fallen in love and in 1831 married a peasant farmer, Soren Pedersen (sometimes the surname of Skaade was appended because he spent most of his early childhood in this area of Aarhus). They started a family right away with the advent of Karen in 1832. Some family stories speculate that Karen stayed in her father's home while her friends were getting married and having babies of their own because her mother needed her. Others say she was nursing a broken heart. One cloudy memory of a long-ago conversation between my father's mother and my mother (who had her own Scandinavian roots) suggests that Karen may have lost a fiancé during the revolutions that rendered Denmark a constitutional monarchy. The loss of lives and dreams may have been worth it: The 1849 constitution ending absolute monarchic rule accorded Danish men the right to vote; it gave every child the right to a public education; it allowed citizens to elect representatives to parliament. In comparison to many nineteenth-century people, Danish men and women enjoyed many liberal freedoms, including the rights of free speech, assembly, and choice of religion.

But in the Sorensen household, the old ways prevailed. This became clear when a missionary from The Church of Jesus Christ of Latter-day Saints (nicknames include LDS and Mormon) came to the door of the half-timbered wattle-and-daub house. According to Norwegian American historian Helge Seljaas, most Nordic people of the 1850s believed that the Mormon missionaries were American degenerates, "agents sent out to lure young Scandinavian girls to join harems in Utah." Before heading out to work the fields, Soren gave his instructions for family safety, and Ane Magrette agreed to prevent the Mormon demons from entering their home.

Regardless of her mother's response to the missionary at her doorstep, Karen took interest in this stranger, touched by the private sun shining from the missionary's face, his enthusiasm radiating despite the hunger and exposure that marked those early missionaries. They traveled "without purse or scrip," having been instructed to rely entirely on the hand of God via the good will of others. I can imagine Ane Magrette shooing the young man away while Karen caught his eye and beckoned over her mother's shoulder — both women tall like all the women on my father's side — miming that the missionary should meet her behind the barn. Karen would have stuffed her feet into wooden shoes and tossed cheese and kippers and bread into a rucksack before slogging across the yard to the pigpen, where she offered provisions to the missionary. Hers would have been a significant kindness, for the missionary faced a daily choice of whether to cut peat to earn his bread or do his missionary work and trust in the Lord to provide. If he was as devoted as were most early missionaries, the young man — having been ordained, like all other male Latter-day Saint missionaries, to the priesthood office of elder — delivered his message before satisfying his hunger, launching into the story of young Joseph Smith in Palmyra, New York, who had been told by an angel to dig from the Hill Cumorah near his parents' home a set of engraved golden plates, which he later translated into the *Book of Mormon*. The missionary held up an abbreviated version of the book, calling it new scripture to guide God's people in these, the last days of the earth.

When Karen risked helping the Mormon missionary, knowing how angered her staunchly Lutheran father would be, she was poised to join a tide of emigrants irresistibly drawn from home to pursue spiritual and earthly adventures. She was ripe to embrace a renewed version of Christ that held the promise of a new life. Her father, an apprentice farmer, had married into a well-to-do family, and now he struggled miserably to provide for a wife who had been raised in comfort. As Soren did what he could to improve their circumstances, Ane dreamed of a better life while she embroidered tapestries and edged linens in lace fit for kings. Soren taught his family to rise before dawn and work well past dusk, a practice he continued for years on end, searching for a means to alter his plight as a tenant farmer. Ane taught her children to crave knowledge and truth and beauty. No immediate end of this dichotomy was in sight, although Karen and her siblings were well educated in the Lutheran school system. The status quo tends to prevail; even though the Danish constitution promised a better life, the aristocracy fulfilled their promises at a snail's pace.

When the Sorensen family first learned of the Mormon movement, they may have also heard that the Restored Gospel of Jesus Christ would usher in a new era for women—a lifting of the curse of Eve so that the daughters of God could embrace birthrights of agency and dignity. Certainly they had heard rumors that The Church of Jesus Christ of Latter-day Saints allowed polygamy by arguing that every worthy woman had the right to become "a mother in Israel." During this post-bellum period, the number of marriageable women may have surpassed the number of marriageable men in Denmark, as so often happens in the aftermath of war, especially one that significantly reduces a country's size. I wondered if Karen, who must have felt her childbearing years passing too quickly, had found this aspect of the Church promising in a pragmatic sense. But certainly she had been compelled by faith to make the dramatic change in her circumstances, for fascination outstripped her sense of duty as a daughter of Denmark, and passionate conviction displaced the ingrained patterns of her youth—obedience, honed by a stern father, and allegiance, shaped by the Lutheran culture that had educated her. When she announced her intention to be baptized into the Church, her father ordered her from the house and banished her from the family. She could return, he told her, only when she recovered from this foolishness.

Did he give her time to collect her hat, her shawl, her boots? Or was she exposed to the harsh elements, cast out in her wooden clogs, wearing only her woolen *skorte* and *strikke* (knitted) *bluse*? I can see her now, craning her neck to study the farmhouse set in its frozen niche before she turned toward the town of Aarhus, on the Jutland Peninsula. She was willing to make her way from there to Copenhagen, if necessary, to pursue her new faith. Once her mind was made up, Karen did not waver, a characteristic that would prove—as I know all too well—both blessing and curse.

The missionaries had told her where the Aarhus meetings were being held along with strict instructions to keep the location to herself. Now homeless, Karen attended those meetings and turned for help to fellow members, who welcomed her with arms wide open. Young Karen was probably pretty in the Danish way: platinum hair, high cheekbones, light-blue eyes. She was no stranger to hard work and applied herself in the homes of other converts who sheltered her. Because she had benefited from Denmark's compulsory education law, she could tutor children and keep household accounts. She could cook, clean house, and scrub laundry alongside any woman. And she could milk cows, cultivate crops, and chop wood alongside any man. At night, in a cot by the kitchen fire, she may have had access to the household's collection of missionary-distributed literature: the Church's periodical known as *Skandinaviens Stjerne*, a Danish translation of the *Book of Mormon* (in 1851, it became the first foreign-language edition of the scripture) and *Bible Reference*.

Karen was not alone in being rejected by family and culture. As historian William Mulder notes, Denmark's new constitutional freedoms permitted religious dissent, paving the way for Mormon missionaries, but culturally ancient ways died hard, especially among the old guard. Brutal reprisals taught Scandinavian Latter-day Saints to cluster in secret. Many idealistic, educated young Danes, repulsed by their parents' habits of drinking to excess and acquiring goods with Viking lust, were attracted to the saintly demeanor of the clean-living saints who trusted in God for the means to live. As young people have always done, the young Danes took identity from opposition; they rejected the practice of eating uncooked meat and deplored their parents' focus on material wealth. They were happy to spurn alcohol, coffee, tea, and tobacco. According to Peder Christian Geertsen's autobiography, Scandinavians had never experienced the sweet humility of kneeling in prayer with their brethren until they embraced The Restored Gospel of Jesus Christ.

The new saints burned with hope and religious fervor; they were headed for the Promised Land. But Nordic social historians such as Seljaas, memoirs by such community leaders as Sven Aarhus, and the journals of early missionaries such as Erastus Snow indicate that the rapid spread of Mormonism alarmed Scandinavian governments and power brokers, who sent constables with billy clubs and ropes to subdue effulgent converts and return them to their families. Hence saints were compelled to whisper prayers and testimonies in hidden groves and sheds and to gather at ponds and freezing fjords to baptize converts beneath the light of moon and stars.

Missionaries were particularly at risk, subject to harassment and incarceration, because the Lutheran Church exercised enormous influence on the community and because Mormon beliefs aroused the ire of stolid Danes. Constables sometimes arrested those Danish saints who remained adamant in their faith. To avert this, converts' families would go to great lengths to intervene — just as do parents of children who join communes and cults or who become addicted to drugs in modern times. Often a convert who had been cast out would be coaxed to visit home, only to be restrained by parents and siblings while friends and family took part in a tableau revealing how converts had been misled by devil Mormons. But these tactics only spurred the movement. As the fledgling Church continued to grow, Lutheran ministers showed up in the town square or at clandestine Mormon meetings to offer brandy while they preached openly against The Church of Jesus Christ of Latter-day Saints. Such affronts seemed to fuel the young church's growth.

Most Scandinavians were disgusted by rumors of polygamy and outraged by saints' touting modern scriptures, living prophets, and plural marriage. Some claimed that saints spurned the Bible and engaged in orgies. Sven Aarrestad, well-known member of the Storting (the Norwegian parliament) and future minister of agriculture, tried to dissuade his brother, Torkel, from joining the Latter-day Saints: "With your knowledge, I cannot understand what you see in such twaddle as these Saints teach . . . . If you had become a Catholic, Methodist, or Baptist, I could have given you my blessing . . . but these horrendous Saints who do not deserve to be called Christians! How could you vilify yourself, your wife and children, and your entire family in such a manner?" Torkel's father gave him a parting message that echoed the curse Karen heard from her own father: "I would rather see you dead than . . . united with that people."

Scandinavian Latter-day Saints often gathered at firesides in homes, a candle illuminating pages of scripture telling of an ancient Israelite family who fled Jerusalem in about 600 BC, just before the fall of the temple. They followed their father, Lehi, who had prophesied that Jerusalem would fall, and that God had promised them a new land. The missionary conducting the meeting might have raised his eyes from the page and proclaimed that this very congregation of Latter-day Saints had been called to gather in that new land, now called America, to build the city of God.

Perhaps the mob found them at this moment of inspiration, breaking the windows and tearing down the door and dragging the Latter-day Saints into the street where they were excoriated verbally and physically. Men were beaten, women mocked as harlots, and buildings set on fire. Such experiences turned the converts more fervently toward Zion, where, they believed, all lived in harmony and, as the LDS scripture promised, "there were no poor among them."

The concept of Zion reflected Joseph Smith's conviction that "man is that he might have joy" which dovetailed beautifully with his revelation of the afterlife: a three-tiered eternity including the celestial kingdom for those who practiced celestial marriage, the terrestrial kingdom for good Christians everywhere, and the telestial kingdom for the rest. Everyone would have a share in paradise except a few benighted "sons of perdition." The prospect of joy appealed greatly to people living in a cold, dark land where everything remained difficult to come by. In the vast country of America, men could go west to homestead property among other self-reliant beings beyond the taint of politics and where freedom of religion could include The Restored Gospel of Jesus Christ. There, the utopia of Zion would be within reach. Convinced that the people of the earth were living in "the last dispensation of time," Karen felt an urgency shared by many converts to embrace the promise of everlasting life among the saints of God before it was too late for her and too late for the world.

The Saints called each other brother and sister and pooled their means as one big family. The missionaries told them about the great organization of Latter-day Saints in Utah, where everyone donated his or her resources and the bishop divided them according to need. The system promised safety and abundance, acceptance of individuality — always important to the Scandinavian people — and the preservation of family as an eternal entity. As Karen listened to the new scripture, whether in English or Danish, her conviction deepened, and she yearned to come to Zion. But she could not bear the thought of leaving her family behind; she longed to share the gospel and the dream of eternal family with her parents and siblings. She met secretly with her mother and arranged for the missionaries to visit while her father was working in the fields. Within three years of Karen's conversion, Ane Magrette entered the moonlit waters of baptism, and her younger children soon followed. When Ane Magrette and her children began to walk the four miles to attend Sunday meetings at the tiny house in Aarhus (which, once persecutions abated, would be rented by the Church for years to come), Soren blamed Karen for his family's defection, which deepened the rift between them.

At this point, Karen would not have returned home even had her father allowed it. Driven by something more than traditional Danish aspirations, she reached for the prospect of heaven on Earth embodied in a desert city in the North American West. After fasting and prayer, Karen decided she would journey to Utah even if she had to give up her family.

From 1854, when Karen was baptized, to 1859, when she left Denmark, she and other converts suffered increasing persecution. Mobs shattered hundreds of windowpanes, broke down dozens of doors, and set barns and homes on fire. The marauders ravaged meetings where sacred ordinances such as baptisms and weddings were in process. With each new outrage, Karen renewed her commitment to emigrate and finally, at one meeting, declared her intention. Apparently, it met with encouragement, because she immediately made plans to travel to Utah.

Because the gathering of the Saints fulfilled one of the prophetic doctrines of the Church, faithful members in Utah Territory actively supported emigration to the Salt Lake Valley. Church authorities mapped routes, booked ships, and organized wagon trains. They lent money to be paid back once impoverished immigrants had established themselves in Zion. Immigration statistics indicate that during the 1850s, more Scandinavian women than men emigrated because of the Church. In the nineteenth century, Nordic peoples made up more than half of all Latter-day Saint immigrants, and of these roughly sixty percent were women. Because males had formerly swelled the ranks of emigrants, the Swedish government studied the phenomenon and concluded that women were more interested in religion than were men. But the Church's Perpetual Emigration Fund (PEF) — which provided interim financial assistance, careful travel plans, and reliable guidance — attracted single women, who may have decided that their chances of suitable marriage would be considerably improved in Zion and who typically had more difficulty securing means and traveling alone than did single men.

Homeless, cast out by her father, persecuted by her fellow citizens, Karen was one of those women most eager to partake of the PEF. She may have encouraged her mother to partake of the Fund as well, in order to emigrate without Soren's consent, but Ane remained with her husband, praying that he would have a change of heart. Karen prepared for her journey to the new world where she would make a home for herself and one day receive her mother and brothers and sisters — perhaps even her recalcitrant father. But then her plans were suddenly obstructed.

Always beset with social and political controversies, the Perpetual Emigration Fund had been dealt a blow by the 1856 tragedy of the Willie and Martin Handcart Companies that were trapped by early snow in the Rocky Mountains of Wyoming. News of the many saints who starved or froze to death traveled across land and sea, calling the program into serious question by prospective immigrants, captains of the handcart companies, and the general public.

In addition, the Utah War had handicapped Mormon commerce, and a worldwide economic crisis prevented Church leaders from securing loans. In October 1857, Brigham Young froze the troubled emigration program.

The PEF had allowed thousands of impoverished immigrants to relocate in the new world and should have been self-sustaining. According to immigrants' agreement with the Church, PEF beneficiaries would cross the seas and the American continent to establish livelihoods in the Rocky Mountain West; then they would manifest their faith and gratitude by sponsoring more immigrants through the PEF. Single women were expected to require more help than were men to complete the cycle and thus endured less pressure to pay it forward. But many immigrants reneged on their agreement with the Church. Some grew disenchanted and lost their faith en route; others simply played the system, abandoning the Church and going on to the gold fields of California. Some decided they didn't want to start their new lives in economic and spiritual debt and renounced their faith, returning to settle the upper Midwest. When the Perpetual Emigration Fund was frozen, so was the flood of immigration. Brigham Young, distressed that the flow had slowed to a trickle, reversed his decision in October 1858. On January 1, 1859, the Perpetual Emigration Fund was galvanized anew, and Church authorities prepared for another wave of European converts.

Karen quickly resumed her plan to emigrate. Before leaving for Copenhagen to begin her voyage across the Atlantic, Karen met with her mother to say goodbye. I imagine their last meeting: Ane Magrette would have stolen away from the house, hoping to avoid a quarrel with Soren. Karen and Ane probably attended church together one last time. By then, persecution of the Saints had diminished somewhat because the congregation could gather in the light of day. In the tiny meetinghouse, mother and daughter sat across the aisle from the men and took the sacrament. I imagine the tight clutch of their hands, the tears filling their eyes as they sang "Come to Zion," Ane Magrette leaning close to whisper that she, too, longed to come to Zion, that she would be patient with Soren as long as possible, but when the children were old enough, they would follow Karen to Utah.

On April 1, 1859, Karen was one of 354 Latter-day Saints aboard the steamer *L.N. Hvidt* when it launched from Copenhagen harbor. Storms wracked the steamship until even the seasoned captain feared that the North Sea would swallow them. But the converts prayed and proclaimed their faith and weathered their way, grateful to arrive at the Grimsby, England, harbor five days later.

The daughter of one Danish convert testified, "[The captain of the steamer] had not yet learned that ships with Mormon members on board never went down." This statement, while not entirely true, does point to a remarkable record of successful voyages during the young Church's immigration period. Although many companies suffered from bouts of illness and malnutrition that took up to ten percent of the lives on board, only one ship of the thousands of vessels carrying Latter-day Saint converts and other passengers went down: In 1855, the *Julia Ann* was making her second voyage from Australia headed for the United States when she splintered on rocks near the Society Islands. Among the thirty-nine passengers on board, twenty-eight were Latter-day Saints; of these, five drowned: two Mormon women and three children.

After landing at Grimsby, Karen traveled with her steamer-mates by rail to Liverpool, where she boarded the *William Tapscott*, a full-rigged packet ship with four masts and sixteen sails. The square stern and billethead announced that the *Tapscott* was a sturdy vessel capable of safely transporting its human cargo across the treacherous deep. Designed for maximum capacity and boasting three decks, the ship was one of the workhorses dominating the cargo and passenger industry of the 1800s. The Scandinavians waited aboard the *Tapscott* for two days until a horde of British and Swiss Latter-day Saints swelled the *Tapscott*'s manifest to 725 passengers, each holding a ticket priced at 4.2 pounds sterling (about $5.50 US in 1859, roughly the equivalent of $170 in 2020).

In 1863, Charles Dickens visited a Mormon emigrant ship, the *Amazon*, expecting to bear testimony against the Latter-day Saints; however, he decided they did not deserve censure. He noted, "Indeed, I think it would be difficult to find eight hundred people together anywhere else and find so much beauty and so much strength and capacity for work among them." This observation represented a reversal of Dickens's assumptions about the Latter-day Saints.

I suspect that after waiting so long, Karen would have been impatient to begin her voyage to Zion, but the *Tapscott's* captain, James B. Bell, decreed they would wait for a storm to pass. She would have tossed and turned in her hammock and repeatedly made her way to the deck so that she could check the progress of the storm. At daybreak on April 11, 1859, Karen emerged early from the dark and crowded steerage to see that the heavy bank of clouds had passed. I imagine her leaning over the railing to breathe the sooty fish-air of Liverpool and smiling, for today they would set sail. The entire ship trembled as sailors dashed about and sharp whistles cut the air. Passengers emerged from below deck, their eyes lit with relief and expectancy. The *William Tapscott* heaved away from the dock and slipped out of Liverpool harbor, while the converts applauded and sang and prayed.

As they sailed into the open ocean, Robert F. Neslen, who had been assigned by Brigham Young to preside over the company of European converts, gathered the passengers together. Swiftly he made clear a system of hierarchies, rules, and protocols keenly reflective of the highly organized Church and making every passenger accountable for certain responsibilities. (This designation of duties would prepare them to assimilate with the industrious Deseret Beehive chosen by Brigham Young to symbolize the Latter-day Saints' working together to build the kingdom of God.) As their ecclesiastical president, Neslen organized the immigrants by creating a hierarchy similar to a Latter-day Saints stake (a diocese). He divided the group into ten wards (like parishes) with five wards of Scandinavians and five wards of British and Swiss members, each with its own ward president. Each of the five-ward groups was assigned one half of the ship, which they kept in pristine condition, to the delight of the ship's crew. The passengers spoke nine different languages, yet Captain Bell and his crew were amazed by how harmoniously the Saints worked together to keep an exceptionally clean and orderly environment.

Such cooperation, hard work, and goodwill rarely occurred on other immigrant crossings. Constructed for efficiently transporting cargo and steerage passengers from the old world to the new, these workhorses carried most of the five million souls who emigrated from Europe to the United States from 1820 to 1860. Ships' proprietors expected to make up to $60,000 a year from each vessel but often made their profit by serving meals that didn't satisfy basic nutritional needs. The Yankee crew, known as packet rats, prided themselves on toughness, ate their hardtack and beans without complaint, and coined the epithet "limey" to mock crewmen of British merchant vessels, who warded off scurvy with a legally ordained dose of lime juice every ten days at sea. The captain and the crew on the *William Tapscott* were as hardened as any group of Yankee sailors, but their cynicism could not dampen the enthusiasm of Latter-day Saints like Karen Sorensen.

Mark Twain, Robert Louis Stevenson, and Rudyard Kipling wrote about nineteenth-century voyages from the United States to Europe and back, but such elite pundits usually enjoyed cabin passage and ate at the captain's table. The crossing of Latter-day Saint emigrants bore only slight resemblance to the voyage Twain described in *Innocents Abroad*. Despite the crew's dour attitudes and clipped commentary, the Saints radiated goodwill; their spirits, it seemed, could not be confined.

Notwithstanding the passengers' enthusiasm, life aboard ship was far from blissful. Too often, the damp, germ-ridden hold with its overpowering stench made those who weren't already sick desperately ill. Healthy steerage passengers, especially those accustomed to seafaring, stayed above deck much of the time. Through family stories, I've heard that Karen took care of steerage passengers who had succumbed to seasickness and other ills. But she sought fresh air regularly on the main deck, where the thrill of open water and the sun beating down stirred dreams of her new life in Utah.

The congregations met on deck at 8:00 every morning and evening for prayer, scripture study, and hymn singing. In the evening, members shared their testimonies, a practice that strengthened their much-needed resolve. They stood, one at a time, as the Holy Spirit moved them; they bore witness to the truthfulness of the Restored Gospel of Jesus Christ and expressed their conviction about joining The Church of Jesus Christ of Latter-day Saints. Some might have told of hardships in Denmark, such as the North Jutland bricklayer who lost his job because he had held Church gatherings in his employer's brickyard and broke holes through iced-over clay pits to perform baptisms. Others might have told of dreams and visions foretelling this very journey. Once religious obligations were met, the Saints lingered to dance, play musical instruments, or recite literature. They shared ethnic stories and poetry and bits of Shakespeare. They drew upon more modern sources as well, justifying their entertainment by referring to the Thirteenth Article of Faith drawn up by Joseph Smith, who quotes the apostle Paul in his admonition that whatsoever things are honest, just, pure, lovely, and of good report would be included in Saints' observance. They read or retold Charles Dickens's stories on the moonlit decks of the *Tapscott*, where Karen also discovered the dark cloud of slavery cast across America during a retelling of Harriet Beecher Stowe's *Uncle Tom's Cabin*, which had been published a half-dozen years before and now galvanized America's conscience.

A day or two after setting sail, a storm threw seas across the deck, and the congregation went below to hold their meetings. Despite the rigors of cleanliness imposed by the Latter-day Saints, the nether regions of the ship held odiferous cargoes, including live goats, sheep, and cows. These, combined with the smells emitted by seasick souls in hammocks strung in the space called between decks, could unsettle even Karen's steady stomach. To distract herself, she may have focused her attention on a young sailor named Mads Peder Rasmussen.

The idea of romance at sea, even under such inauspicious conditions, made me wildly curious about Mads. I wondered if Karen had known him in Denmark but suspect that the ship voyage allowed their first meeting. The prospect of getting to know him got me rummaging through old boxes, searching for the notes from my long-ago interviews with Aunt Rhea. I remembered her stately 1890s house in what was left of rural Draper, Utah, and Aunt Rhea, whose dark beauty contrasted sharply with my father's platinum hair and light eyes. Growing up, they had been regarded as twins because they were born three months apart to my Grandfather Harvey's plural wives. Aunt Rhea's mother, Charlotte, died in childbirth when Rhea was four years old; the latter often brought tears to my grandfather's eyes because she reminded him of her departed mother.

When I went to see her in the course of conducting research for my first book, Aunt Rhea's hair was shot with gray and her dark eyes glowed with the fervor of those who seek to enlighten the dismal masses. She ushered me into a parlor furnished with heavy mahogany pieces draped in lace: lace curtains at the windows, lace doilies on the backs and arms of overstuffed chairs and sofas, lace tablecloths and filigreed picture frames. She answered some of my questions about my father as a boy, laughing at her memories. Then her eyes burned brighter as if she had just remembered what I had come to learn: She had written "Mother Evelyn's" story and the story of Great-grandmother Mary Catrena Rasmussen Clark as well. She had drawn from the stories Grandmother Evelyn had told her, the stories told by Mary Catrena's favorite brother, George Henry, who had written his own ancestral account, and the stories bequeathed on her of Karen, most of which, she told me with eyes twinkling, were housed in Great-grandfather Arthur's biography. Aunt Rhea chattered on and on. She gave me advice. She promised to send me a copy of her book when it was published. But other than relating the story of Karen and Mads pulling a handcart and tending oxen together, she never said a word about my great-great-grandfather.

Again I consulted the Clark biography to read about Mads running away to sea and that George Henry had known his father, Mads Peder Rasmussen. When I found George Henry, I also found mention of his namesake, nephew George Hammond Clark, a son of Mary Catrena. I returned to the Utah History Research Center again and again over several years. There I shivered or perspired, according to the season, as its musty volumes breathed back at me recalcitrant revelations, mere tatters of Karen's life. Some accounts were in the writer's original script, ornate to a fault, almost indecipherable.

Fortunately, in 2014, I found replicas and typewritten versions of these stories on the ancestral website sponsored by The Church of Jesus Christ of Latter-day Saints, FamilySearch.org, which had shared information with other ancestral organizations to make family histories available online. The Georges' accounts corroborate the Arthur Benjamin Clark biography that as a young man, Mads Peder Rasmussen had run away to evade mandatory conscription into the Danish army and had become a sailor serving on the *William Tapscott*. For a time, I had imagined him as a handsome swashbuckler with a cutlass tucked into his belt and a red scarf tying back his long locks, lithely climbing nets and swabbing decks as he eyed my prim grandmother. I imagined that he drank grog and told wicked stories, and that Karen, intending from the start to properly civilize him, set about converting him to the Restored Gospel. And then I wondered whether this sailor had any prior inkling that on this particular voyage of the *William Tapscott* he would meet the woman he would one day describe as the love of his life and who would alter his seafaring course forever.

Mads may have already noticed Karen before he worked up the courage to speak to her; more likely, given the circumstances, she had been trying to attract his attention. His photographs reveal a handsome, well-groomed man with muttonchop sideburns and large, warm eyes. Family records describe him as a slender man of nearly six feet.

I imagined their first formal meeting on a clear night, the young sailor scanning the deck as Karen and other Scandinavian converts emerged from steerage for their prayer meeting. She would have caught and held his eye, giving back a gaze of capability and youthful wisdom. Karen and her dashing new convert must have reveled in the prospect of the Restored Gospel, that their mortal existence would yield eternal exaltation and worlds without end if they fulfilled the commandments. The sun would have slipped below the horizon, allowing stars to peer at the full-rigged packet on the great sea. The sight would have stirred their blood, just as the nightly meetings stirred the fire of the Holy Spirit and reminded them that only those who married would reach the highest kingdom in heaven. The Church doctrines that fanned their spiritual fervor toward celestial marriage also urged reserve, despite the electrified air between them.

Yet if they went below decks to seek shelter from the fierce storm that broke three days into the voyage, they may have huddled near the goats to absorb their warmth. Dim as the light may have been, amid the sour smell of manure and the sweet bleating of a kid, it would have been difficult to ignore one another's penetrating looks. The storm pitched the *Tapscott* to and fro, but according to family stories handed down to my father from his mother, Karen wasn't prone to panic and was known for her strong constitution and firm resolve. Mads, the seasoned sailor, would have liked that. He led her above deck to watch the wild waves, the sea rolling in great mountains that subsided into gentle hills as the storm abated, unveiling an oversized moon.

The pair had little in common other than their Danish heritage and their new faith, but they didn't need more: they were young and moonstruck, and undeniably felt the call of an adventure grander than the sea. Their religion urged them to serve God's Plan by creating an eternal family bonded in infinite progression, populating worlds without end. On another ship in different company, they might have waited until they reached New York, or they might have postponed their nuptials until reaching Salt Lake City, there to be sealed "for time and all eternity" in the Endowment House. But aboard the *Tapscott*, marriages were being negotiated left and right, to the delight of Church authorities and the ship's captain, James Bell. There may have been a contest afoot, for weddings were not infrequent on Mormon immigrant ships. By making marriages of relationships that might otherwise invite sin, mid-ocean unions protected the souls of those with celestial glory in their sights. Fellow Saints may have urged young couples into marriage by reminding them that they might drown or take sick or shipwreck; they didn't want to miss out on their divine inheritance, did they? Mads and Karen disregarded their limited knowledge of one another, joined hands, and plunged toward immortality. Theirs was one of nineteen marriages solemnized on board during that voyage.

Of course, their marriage introduced complications. Did Mads give up his position on the *Tapscott* and simply jump ship, a practice not uncommon for sailors who had no intention of returning to their home port? Or had he planned all along that this would be his final voyage and was he simply working his way across to pay for passage? His listing as Sailor on the masthead indicated nothing more than his general occupation. Perhaps he was strictly a passenger this voyage, helping only when needed because he knew how. The possibilities, I supposed, were many. In any case, their romance blossomed rapidly enough that they were married on board and left the ship as husband and wife.

As immigrant crossings went, the *Tapscott* death toll was low: The demise of an elderly Swedish woman who was ailing before the journey began was counterbalanced by the births of two babies. A quick passage with few storms, so little illness, and one death was rare on the packet ships, which jeopardized lives through crowding, spoiled provisions, and inadequate crews. Even the large and full-rigged *William Tapscott* had been written up for violations leading to the deaths of sixty-five passengers on one voyage — a full ten percent of steerage. But no negative reports characterized the spring voyage of 1859.

The storms were blessedly few, as were the accidents. The *Tapscott*'s living cargo reached New York Harbor in record time — only thirty-three days at sea, from April 11 to May 14 — and anchored overnight in New York Harbor. According to Robert Neslen, doctors and immigration officials pronounced them the healthiest and best-disciplined passengers ever to arrive on their watch. As recorded in the journal of British convert and emigrant Henry Hobbs (spelled Hobbes in some records), the harbor was crowded with ships: a man-of-war, and other large transports, including the *Commonwealth* and the *Metropolis. The New York Times* reported that nearly four thousand emigrants had arrived that day, docking in ships from Liverpool, Le Havre, and Bremen. Some immigrant ships had been denied permission to disembark passengers because of illness, including one bearing smallpox that was sent on to Halifax. Hearing this report, the Latter-day Saints thanked heaven for their safe voyage and good health. The next morning a ferry took them to Castle Garden, where they slept on the floor of immigration headquarters. Hobbs, who would keep a comprehensive journal of his trek to Zion, was pleased to note that the New York newspapers did write-ups on their company.

The New York Times mentioned the arrival of 726 Mormon immigrants aboard the *William Tapscott*, conceding, "They are a better class than the average European emigrants." The *Times* devoted most of its pages to the expansion of the Austro-Italian War, the increasingly incendiary slavery issue, Susan B. Anthony's stump for woman's rights, and President Buchanan's ineffectual response to Mormon insolence in Utah.

The *New York Herald* gave a more extensive report of the *Tapscott* arrival, including a list of immigrants documented as disembarking at Castle Garden. My great-great-grand-parents are listed together, first Karen Rasmussen and then Mads Rasmussen, a couple. There, on that page, lay proof of my American roots. Does it seem surprising that I was elated? Consider what such evidence can mean to the illicit child of an extralegal family: I was sixty-three before I was able to obtain a birth certificate. To get it, I had to prove that my father was indeed my father—without DNA, as he'd been murdered thirty-five years earlier. Instead, I provided court documents that listed me as his daughter in the 1991 civil suit against the woman who killed him. The jury had awarded our family $52.5 million in damages we did not try to collect; we were satisfied that the judgment would discourage the murderer from making money from books, appearances, or anything else relating to her story. Beyond sweet justice and granting our family legitimacy that never before seemed possible, the suit would prove valuable in a much larger arena. Our attorney would tell me years later how in 1997 it served as paradigm and precedent for the Goldman family civil suit that kept O. J. Simpson from capitalizing on the murders of Nicole Simpson and Ron Goldman. I have collected such shreds of citizenship throughout my life, as proof of my right to be.

President Robert Neslen wrote to Brigham Young and later reported in the Church newspaper, *Millennial Star*, that authorities pronounced the *Tapscott* immigrants "the best disciplined and most agreeable company that ever arrived at [this] port." Feeling duly welcomed, the company prepared to board the steamboat *Isaac Newton* (which would burn to embers while steaming along the Hudson four years later, killing nine and scalding many more). The *Herald* article remarked on the astonishing amount of extra baggage carried by "people of their class"—some fifty thousand pounds. "Considering the expense of transportation in Europe . . . and the charges going west . . . it is presumed that the Saints had held on to the valuables and heirlooms from father to son, etc., to enrich the valleys of the mountains." But before the *Isaac Newton* could head up the Hudson River, discord broke out when gentile immigrants bound for Albany settled in among the Latter-day Saints, thus raising consternation among the Church leaders present. Responsible for the immigrants' wellbeing, these brethren were understandably wary. Persecution followed Saints wherever they went, and among the immigrants were many young single women. According to the *Herald* article, a "chief elder" cleared the steamer, "after which the faithful boarded at the call of their names; then the outsiders were quartered in another part of the vessel. This separating of the sheep from the goats detained the *Isaac Newton* a full hour."

The segregating of Latter-day Saints from unbelievers reflects Church leaders' concern for the converts' dignity and safety; fallout from "the Mormon Rebellion," as some pundits in the east called the Utah War, had reached the East Coast. The emigration organizer for The Church of Jesus Christ, George Q. Cannon, also took into account the mounting discord over slavery (nearly a decade of contention in "Bleeding Kansas" would culminate that July with the Wyandotte Constitution outlawing slavery, and in October with John

Brown's unsuccessful raid on the federal armory at Harpers Ferry). Cannon directed Robert Neslen to take his immigrants north instead of traveling the usual route directly across the heartland. Upon reaching Albany, the company boarded a train bound for the Canadian border. I think of Karen and Mads staring out at Niagara Falls, amazed by the power and beauty of this vast continent, yet fighting a wave of nostalgia for the great waters of their homeland as they thundered across the suspension rail bridge into Canada. I felt Karen's apprehension at passing over a border she'd never intended to cross, and then realized I was projecting, saddling her with my own life-long angst. Somehow Karen's crossing recalled the panic I'd felt as a child stealing into Mexico with my family as the government rounded up children of polygamy and took them from their parents, an anxiety that attended me into adulthood each time I left the US until the day I secured my birth certificate.

Rocked to sleep on the carriage boards of the train, the immigrants were awakened by crowds at one station after another, people gawking and shouting questions about spiritual wifery and Mormon scriptures and why gathering in the West was so important—was Brigham Young trying to start his own kingdom out there?

At Windsor, Ontario, they crossed back into the United States and over the Detroit River where they met alternately jeering and cheering crowds in Detroit and Chicago. They traveled to Quincy, Illinois, not far from the city of Nauvoo, where my great-great-great-grandfather Isaac Allred and his family had lived among the other Saints in the 1840s. During the brief layover in Quincy, some converts made pilgrimage to the Carthage, Illinois, jail where their prophet, Joseph Smith, had been assassinated in 1844. But most of the immigrants stayed inside the train, fearing the volatile crowds. Henry Hobbs wrote of Quincy, "We spent the day under cover . . . . In the evening went . . . for a swim in the Mississippi. There was a very rough crowd down at the station. Some were returning from Pikes Peak . . . disappointed in getting gold. I hear thousands more are returning."

According to accounts from immigrants and Church leaders, the Saints left Quincy to board the packet steamer *Saint Mary*, passing near Mark Twain's childhood home on the way to St. Joseph, Missouri. Hobbs wrote, "A strong guard was appointed to keep watch. We had some rough customers to deal with . . . . St. Joseph is a flourishing town. Slaves are sold here." Hobbs explained that while they made some berths aboard the packet steamer, several women oppressed by the heat went on deck to sleep.

> In the night while I was on guard I heard a row & made for it; when I got there I found the sailors arguing with some of the Danish. One threatened to use his knife. I immediately went for President Neslen & he came and spoke as one having authority[;] he said they could not [try] their Missouri tricks with us & if they wanted a row we were on hand.

I can't help wondering whether my great-great-grandfather Mads Rasmussen, a young sailor accustomed to brawling, was among those Danish men poised to fight.

The next day, the company steamed along the Missouri River to Florence, Nebraska, where the company was organized into temporary branches, with priesthood leaders appointed to supervise the welfare of everyone encamped on the riverbank. The Robert Neslen Company was divided into five groups, three of pioneers who pulled handcarts and two made up primarily of wagons. The route had been drawn up by George Q. Cannon specifically for this immigrant company arriving from Europe on the eve of the Civil War. Although six Mormon handcart companies had crossed the Atlantic and the heartland, the Neslen party was proud to be the first to take the route through Ontario to Florence. They felt themselves to be bona fide pioneers, blazing a trail that others could follow to skirt the impending Civil War.

By the time they reached Florence, Karen and Mads must certainly have heard stories of earlier handcart companies. When Brigham Young was inspired to sponsor immigrants pulling handcarts, the first success built enthusiasm for another. Two more handcart companies crossed the Great Plains and the Rocky Mountains with few mishaps, all in the spring and early summer of 1856. In their zeal to reach Zion, the fourth and fifth groups set sail late that same year, having been detained by economic factors; they were further delayed at the staging areas. Known as the Willie and the Martin Handcart Companies, these immigrant groups poised to cross the Rocky Mountains perilously late in the season. The Latter-day Saints elders in charge were divided about whether to commence the journey or winter in Nebraska. Immigrants unfamiliar with the terrain and weather left the decision to those leaders who had already made the crossing. Three of the four experienced brethren urged them on, but Brother Levi Savage spoke against the plan, insisting that a company harboring old people and little children would suffer sickness and death. When the majority voted against him, Savage acknowledged, "[S]eeing you are to go forward, I will go with you . . . will work with you . . . will suffer with you . . . and if necessary, I will die with you."

Franklin D. Richards, who had been released from his calling as mission president in Great Britain, arrived in Florence, Nebraska, just in time to launch the last wagons of the Martin Company, on August 25. He promised to ride ahead with his entourage and alert Brigham Young to expect them. Richards stopped to assure Captain James G. Willie that he would arrange for suppliers from Salt Lake to meet the company at the continental divide known as South Pass. But as Brother Savage predicted, the results of the late launch were disastrous: Many would lose their lives; the survivors gave up fingers, feet, and limbs to early winter snows. Unlike the Donner and Fremont parties, they did not fight for supplies or eat each other; in fact, they sacrificed for one another and died believing they were headed for celestial glory. Wallace Stegner wrote, "Perhaps their suffering seems less dramatic because handcart pioneers bore it meekly, praising God instead of fighting for life with the ferocity of animals."

On October 4, when Franklin Richards arrived in Salt Lake City with news that two more handcart companies were stranded on the plains, the Church Conference was about to convene. Brigham Young proposed this text for his sermon to the Saints: "To get them here." He reiterated: "This is my religion; the dictation of the Holy Ghost . . . to save the people [on the plains]." Among the many responsive Latter-day Saints was my great-great-granduncle Reddick Allred, who joined a relief party headed by Captain George D. Grant. Reddick loaded his wagon with supplies and drove his team into a bliz-zard so fierce he could not open his eyes. When the relief party reached South Pass, where the continent divides east-flowing and west-flowing waters, they expected to find the Willie Company, which had been ahead of the Martin Company by a few days, but no trace of either company could be found. Captain Grant instructed Reddick and others to stay there and guard the supplies while Grant led an advance party up the Sweetwater River in search of the handcart companies.

As one storm passed and another descended, the two men who'd stayed with Reddick decided it was foolish to remain. Perhaps they believed that the handcart companies were win-tering somewhere, or that everyone had died. In any case, the two men took several wagons and turned back toward Salt Lake City; as they met wagons coming out of Salt Lake, they turned each one back—in all, seventy-seven wagons that could have helped. But Reddick refused to give up his post. He guarded the supply wagons and slaughtered the seven head of beef they'd acquired in Fort Bridger, hanging the quarters from trees where they would keep out of reach of animals. He wrote in his journal about the conflict he felt as snow blinded him and pleurisy crippled his lungs and wrung him out, but he hung on, not knowing when or whether the rescuers would show up with the handcart pioneers.

Meanwhile, Captain Grant dispersed express teams to search for the handcart companies. One express party member climbed a ridge and left a wooden sign, which alerted handcart company outriders Captain Willie and Joseph Elder to the whereabouts of the rescue party. Gradually the blizzard abated enough that rescuers could reach one survivor and then another. But many of the Saints had frozen to death where they'd huddled around campfires or lain side by side, their fingers intertwined. The express contingent shared their meager stores, then helped members of the Willie Company scale the steep five miles of Rocky Ridge. Others waited at the bottom of the ravine surrounded by the bodies of those who had died attempting to cross the ridge. Grant sent word to Reddick Allred, who took six wagons and braved fifteen miles through another blizzard, descending from South Pass to Rock Creek Hollow. There he saw the immigrants approach with their backs to him "in such a hard west wind that they could not travel facing the drifting snow." He fed and clothed the living from his supplies and helped them to shelter in the wagons.

In his journal, Reddick described the frozen bodies of those who hadn't survived: "[D]ead and dying lay over the camp in the drifting snow that was being piled in heaps by the gale, thus burying the dead." According to family legend, Reddick's resolve earned him the nickname of "the bulldog." He considered his nightmares a small price to pay for saving so many lives. But the thought of those lives lost—more than 200 of the 980 pioneers in those companies died — continued to haunt Great-great-granduncle Reddick and other Saints across generations, serving as an example of supreme sacrifice for the Gospel of Jesus Christ.

⌘   ⌘   ⌘

I wonder, as Karen and Mads looked across the Missouri River and the Great Plains, what they thought of their odds against bad weather, prairie fires, and Sioux Indians. They might face swollen rivers and muddy roads, bears and wolves in the formidable Rocky Mountains, and, possibly, an early killing snow. Karen began to feel the full weight of her choice, and perhaps realized the costs of agency. Mads felt it, too, the irrevocable responsibility of what lay ahead — not least, for him, the deliberate life he'd committed to — *if* they made it to Utah. Did doubt overwhelm them, if only for a moment, before faith put it on a leash and made it lie down?

CHAPTER 2

Crossing the Plains

W E HAD OUR SHARE of suffering when I was growing up. Because of polygamous roundups, as the press called them (or raids, as we called them), and because my father had promised to stop living plural marriage if that action would parole him from prison, we children under five years old were often whisked from our beds to sleep on basement floors in friends' houses or in the back seats of cars headed across borders into another state or nation.

When we cried or complained about homesickness, my father regaled us with Grandmother Karen's story; he implied that we could not possibly pay greater prices than those rendered by this ancestor who endured everything from storm-tossed seas to fierce rattlesnakes and survived so that we might be raised in Zion. In a sense, I think he meant Karen's life to be that of a female allegory for Christ. According to my father, the daughter and granddaughter who came after her — the healer, Mary Catrena, and the longsuffering plural wife, Mary Evelyn (my grandmother) — followed the pattern. My father's

half-sister, Rhea Allred Kunz, concurred. So grateful was she
to Evelyn as her other mother that she wrote about Evelyn's
people as if they were her own. According to Rhea, Mads and
Karen shared responsibility for pulling a handcart with their
personal goods (about seventeen pounds' worth) plus their
share of the company's supplies (another 233 pounds), and at
night they hobbled and fed and watered the oxen to pay their
share of the trek, $150 per adult.

At journey's end, when debts were tallied, handcart pioneers were sometimes surprised to find they owed a fee for the
use of the church-owned handcart, of which their personal
belongings had occupied less than 8 percent. Mons Larson,
an immigrant who was part of Robert Neslen's wagon train
before he joined the Neslen Company's advance party, told his
daughter that even those who built their own handcarts with
the intent of using them on their prospective farms discovered that their handcarts became the property of the Perpetual
Emigration Fund as soon as they arrived in Zion. For many,
it was their first experience of the United Order, a communal
system practiced by the early Church, where all was given to
the bishop who divided and distributed it according to need.
This system ensured the young church's survival despite the
ravages of pioneering and persecution and the plagues that
destroyed crops.

The immigrants staged their overland trek from Florence.
Of the five companies under Robert Neslen, George Rowley's
handcart company would leave first, preceded only by a small
forward party organized by Neslen. The latter's own company of wagons and teams would leave last, a full two weeks
later. Mads and Karen must have been anxious as they read-
ied themselves to begin their journey in June 1859. Traveling
more slowly, those pulling handcarts needed an early enough
start to stay ahead of the wagon trains and adverse weather in
the high Rockies. The experiences of other handcart couples

affirm Aunt Rhea's and my father's stories that Karen and Mads would have taken turns pulling and pushing the heavy cart. In the evenings, they would have worked together to tend the company's oxen before they ate or rested. Footsore and weary, handcart immigrants sat to sing and play musical instruments, but having walked an average of fifteen to sixteen miles each day, they didn't do much campfire dancing, as did their wagon-train counterparts.

Official records corroborate Aunt Rhea's and my father's stories about Karen's handcart experience. Karen Sorensen, 27, is listed among 235 immigrants pulling 60 handcarts led by George Rowley, having left the staging area in Nebraska on June 7, 1859. I knew my handcart grandmother was born in 1832. This had to be her, the woman originally listed on the manifests from Copenhagen and later Liverpool as Karen Sorensen: Spinster. Keeping their records straight must have been more important to them than recording her new last name.

On June 9, Rowley's handcart pioneers pursued their arduous trek to Utah in earnest. Leaders knew that the meager supplies (even with six oxen-drawn supply wagons that accompanied them) and heavy carts would spell disaster if the company had not cleared the Rockies by early winter. According to some accounts, worried company commanders sometimes urged the trekkers to a punishing pace of 15.7 miles per day. (Some sources claim an implausible twenty to twenty-five miles per day.)

According to immigrant William Atkin, who wrote an autobiographical sketch and later told his handcart story to the (St. George) *Union* in 1896, the pioneers began their trek in good spirits. Atkin's little brother, Frank, knew all the words to the "Handcart Song" and sang them as they walked, urging everyone to join in the chorus:

Some must push and some must pull
As we go marching up the hill
As merrily on the way we go
Until we reach the valley, oh.

As the days went by, little Frank launched into song less and less eagerly, and eventually the others declined to join in the chorus. One day when asked to sing the "Handcart Song," Frank refused outright. "I will never sing it again," the boy told his family. Atkin reports, "I think he kept his word."

Karen and Mads would have slept in a tent holding ten to eighteen occupants; everyone followed the lights-out and silence orders issued by the tent captain who took his instructions from the captain of a hundred. No one had the energy or inclination to rebel against the schedule, for it was essential to mutual survival. Although they stopped nightly, the men often went on hunting-and-gathering forays while others were sleeping. Foraging would have been difficult, for Latter-day Saint immigrants overlapped with gold rushers and military troops who had cleared the land like a plague of grasshoppers.

Soon after the Rowley Company left Wood River, a band of Sioux stopped them, demanding food. The immigrants gave up a large percentage of their flour and bacon and felt fortunate to keep their scalps. That night, the Sioux clustered around the company's campfire and danced in exotic and frightening displays of power. The handcart company departed at daybreak, but the Sioux followed them on horseback, lassoing their carts and trying to persuade the young women to come away with them. When fancy dancing and intimidation didn't work, they offered buffalo meat and ponies in exchange for the girls, but when these were declined, they sauntered away.

The Saints of the Rowley Company were frightened and hungry by the time they reached Fort Laramie. They had hoped to replenish their supplies, but little was available. The last of their flour was distributed at Devil's Gate, Wyoming — a site significant in the Willie and Martin rescue of 1856. They struggled to feed themselves from the land, gathering berries and tubers where they could. In his diary, immigrant Mathias Nielsen wrote of his gratitude whenever he was able to bring game back to camp. He reports that one night a camp guard smelled a dead animal and drew a bead on a wild creature devouring the carcass; the animal lifted its head just as the guard was squeezing the trigger. Fortunately, the jolt of recognizing one of the members, so starved that he was scavenging like a coyote, diverted the guard's aim.

Before long, some of the company were too starved and worn to go on. Nineteen-year-old Sarah Hancock Beesley, the first wife of Ebenezer Beesley (who would pen more than a dozen Latter-day Saint hymns, found Utah's first and most profitable music store, and eventually lead the world-renowned Mormon Tabernacle Choir), wrote of their delirious joy upon reaching a remote outpost in Wyoming called Big Sandy, where a group of traders, mountaineers, stage drivers, and mail agents had gathered. She writes of her gratitude at being offered breakfast by women attending the mountain men.

But William Atkin observed the situation differently. He reported that "six or eight men, with more whiskey in them than good sound sense," hailed the Saints as they watered their emaciated, bedraggled livestock. One of the mountain men yelled, "We want a wife. Who wants to be a wife?" The mountain men then invited the hungry immigrants to a breakfast of johnny-cake and milk laced with whiskey. Atkin reported, "To our surprise two of our young women stepped out and said they would marry them. One . . . had a lover in our company and they had always appeared affectionate . . . but alas! their starving condition seemed to drive all natural feelings away from them." The other young woman had left her home in Scotland to gather with the Saints, but apparently her blistered feet convinced her to become a mountain man's woman, according to Atkin's account.

In reminiscing with her daughter-in-law, Sarah Beesley reported that the Scottish girl never made it to Zion, and that "she was not the only one who never reached the Valley." But Atkin, who returned to Green River to work for a few months before completing his trek to Zion, reported that both women eventually arrived in the Salt Lake Valley. One brought her mountain man husband along and presumably asked him to convert, while the other reconciled with her Mormon fiancé who forgave and married her.

As the group reached the Green River, they hoped to meet supply wagons from Salt Lake City. But the supply teams hadn't arrived. Captain George Rowley and a companion rode out hoping to find the supply wagons or some other source of food. Meanwhile, people begged from one another, but almost every family was depleted. One newlywed bartered her wedding ring for an extra ration of flour from the captain's wife. The company passed noonday without a meal. The pioneers agreed they must traverse the river's muddy, swirling waters despite their weakened state and sooner rather than later; because the day was waning, they must cross whether Captain Rowley returned or not. But this decision raised ire in one Scots family; they refused to cross before the captain returned.

Another family had left early that morning, striking out ahead of the main company, but they had taken a wrong turn in the road. An outrider found them, but they would not arrive in time to go over with the main company. The river was wide and only about three feet deep, just high enough to wet the axles of the handcarts; however, the swift current and slippery rocks made crossing difficult, especially for those who were trembling after four days without bread. Those who were too weak received help from those who still had strength, and most of the company crossed within two hours. Although a few hours of daylight remained, the company collapsed on the other side of the river, too exhausted to go on. Captain Rowley joined them that night, his saddlebags empty. He approved the killing of a cow; the skinny beast was slaughtered and consumed in a trice, bones and all.

The next morning, they walked four miles southwest alongside the Green River and stopped briefly to rest. A middle-aged woman named Jane Morris Jarvis sat down, and according to Helena Erickson Roseberry, "gave three heavy sighs and died." Sister Jarvis's daughter, Ann Jarvis Stickney, wrote, "If she could only have had bread to eat, she would have lived." The company paused to bury her on the side of the road. Writes Ann, "The sisters were very kind. They washed her and put clean clothes on her and sewed her up tight in a white bed blanket." They put her in the ground, and as soon as the grave was filled they moved on. Ann did not see her mother's grave again.

Sister Jarvis wasn't the only woman who died during this part of the journey. William Atkin writes that around the time Sister Jarvis died, a Sister Mary Jane Shanks had said to Atkin's wife, "Sister, the martyrdom of Joseph and Hyrum was nothing to compare to this." Sister Shanks couldn't keep up with the handcart company, but the exhausted pioneers didn't notice where she fell. Atkin reports that Sister Shanks's body was found some time later, "mostly devoured by wolves." No one knew for sure whether she had died of starvation and exposure or if the wolves had brought her down.

Some members of Neslen's original forward party had been so overcome with hunger and exhaustion that they fell back, hoping for help from the Rowley Company. Rowley Company had little to offer these frontrunners. The mood of despair must have been palpable when Henry Hobbs, who had moved ahead of the larger company, met "a Jentile" [*sic*], a Mr. Dempsey who had set up a camp near the trail. Dempsey invited Hobbs and a few others who had caught up with him to join him for a repast. Dempsey fed the handful of starving pioneers a sumptuous breakfast of bread and butter, ham, boiled beef, milk, and coffee with sugar. Dempsey promised to replenish their supplies when they reached Ham's Fork; they could pay him for 500 pounds of flour, or they could replace his stores before October. Spirits lifted and they continued onward. Just before they reached Ham's Fork, six mule teams crested the hill — the supply wagons at last! But they did not arrive in time to save a Danish mother of five who died during the night.

Once replenished by the supply wagons and uplifted by the encouraging words of Church leaders, the George Rowley handcart company had the strength to complete the last 170 miles of their journey without further incident. On September 4, they reached the Salt Lake Valley; they were able to parade into Zion with flowers in their hair, singing and waving to the Saints who lined the streets to welcome them.

In none of the journals written by members of the George Rowley handcart company did anyone mention my great-great-grandmother Karen, as Sorensen or Rasmussen. Biting back a gnawing disappointment, I reread my copies of the immigration records I had found. I had a photocopy of the yellowed record penned by PEF agent, Asa Calkin, before the *Tapscott* sailed from Liverpool, listing Karen Sorensen, 27, and Mads Peder Rasmussen, 22. They were also listed in the ship's log as being among the nineteen couples wed aboard the *Tapscott*. Then, listed side by side on the beautifully penned immigration record of those aboard the *Tapscott* when it arrived at Castle Garden, New York, were Karen and Mads Peder Rasmussen, both belonging to the Aarhus Conference group of Latter-day Saints who had traveled ensemble from Aarhus, Denmark. But on the latter record was a detail I'd overlooked: Mads's age was listed correctly as 22, but Karen

Rasmussen's age was listed as 24, not the 27 as noted beside the Karen Sorensen of the Rowley company.

How could I have missed the discrepancy when my ancestors' birthdates indicate that Karen was four, almost five years older than Mads? I had that breathless feeling you get when balance is lost and you feel yourself tipping over.

There could be any number of explanations, I told myself. Really a worst-case scenario might be only that Karen was too embarrassed to reveal her true age to her young husband. What difference, she might have wondered, would it make in their new world, where no one else would ever know?

I tried to see the discrepancy dispassionately, to chalk it up to too many records, too many immigrants, so many progeny — the Mormon embarrassment of riches in lists too lush and varied to keep them all in order. But my father had often quoted scripture, emphasizing, "My house is a house of order," and I couldn't leave it alone. The compulsion gave me headaches and woke me from dreams about puzzles I couldn't solve.

Sleeplessness hooked me into further research online. On FamilySearch.org I found new accounts of Mary Catrena and of her brother George's life rendered by grandchildren and great-grandchildren. Then, while double-checking facts, I stumbled across Mads's life story rendered by his daughters Annie, Amanda, and Alice — what daughters were these? I wondered, more startled than I should have been. Other daughters should hardly be surprising to anyone born into a plural family, but what these daughters had to say certainly was. The Other Daughters Rasmussen (ODR, as I'll refer to them for expediency's sake) claimed that young Mads had served as first mate during the *William Tapscott* voyage on which he'd been converted and that Mads was descended from a Danish line of nobles, the Basse family. Here was a discrepancy far greater than the one that led me to it.

If Mads descended from noble blood and was an officer aboard ship, I had to revise my mental picture of the rambunctious sailor who eyed Karen as he swabbed the decks of the *Tapscott*. Instead of a grimy cotton blouse, he would have worn a jacket with epaulets; instead of going barefoot, he'd have worn boots. The long locks that I'd pictured flagged by sea winds would have been tied up and clubbed. The ODR had framed Mads's draft evasion more charitably than had the Clark account. Based on stories Mads had told them, they concluded that from his privileged childhood, Mads had nursed a dream of going to sea. As he reached the age of conscription, instead of giving two years to the army, he simply joined a merchant ship's crew and stayed on, which was why at age twenty-two, Mads was sailing to America on the same ship he'd manned two years prior, about the time he had converted to The Church of Jesus Christ of Latter-day Saints.

The prospect of royal ancestry was nothing new to me. My father claimed to have traced the Allred line to John of Gaunt, and my mother's people tracked family lines to the Stuarts and Farquharsons of Scotland. As a child, I wanted to believe that we descended from royalty, but I'd come to consider the matter of royal lineage a fantasy drawn from poverty, an incentive to lift oneself up and make something more of a miserable or mediocre existence than it can offer in the moment.

But to document their claim to Danish royal blood, the ODR had traced their ancestry through Mads on both his mother's and father's sides and had found various confirmations. And the story they told was radically different from than the one I had always heard from my father. Mads, the ODR asserted, being born of landed gentry, was "a man of some means," which allowed him to purchase a covered wagon and a team of oxen. I wondered if the story of Mads's wealth and nobility was as important to his other families as Karen's handcart story was to mine.

Regardless, I had to admit that the ODR version would explain how Karen's name came to be listed in two separate sub-groups of the Robert Neslen Company. It makes perfect sense that as a recipient of the Perpetual Emigration Fund, Karen Sorensen — a spinster at age 27, cast out and impoverished — would have been assigned to the George Rowley Company of handcarts. Yet if Mads had inherited wealth, marrying him would have instantly elevated Karen's status and mode of travel across the American plains and mountains. That Mads and Karen are listed as traveling with the Robert Neslen Company comprised mostly of wagons drawn by oxen gives credence to the story told by Annie, Amanda, and Alice Rasmussen. Karen's listing in the Rowley Company might be nothing more than the equivalent of today's digital ghost, a record accidentally left unexpunged. As for the legendary handcart pioneer of my father's stories, the focal character of my agency canvas? I felt her dissolving into ectoplasm.

And yet I couldn't be sure. One rainy afternoon, I reexamined a fuzzy document involving Karen's and Mads's emigration. What if the elegantly penned 24 beside Karen Rasmussen's name on the manifest were meant to be a calligraphic 27 and later mistakenly transcribed? Couldn't that, coupled with the differing last names, account for the persisting record of Karen the handcart pioneer?

My father pinned so much on his belief in an ancestral great-grandparent who predisposed him to "suffer all things" and "endure to the end" that he tolerated penury and persecution with humor and courage. I can't be certain that he was wrong; when last I looked, Karen Sorensen was still listed as part of George Rowley's handcart company.

If Karen trekked with the Rowley party, she would have arrived in the Salt Lake Valley on September 4, 1859, eleven days before her husband. Would such a scenario be plausible? How auspicious would such circumstances be for the couple's

future? I conceded that when Robert Neslen arrived in the
Salt Lake Valley on September 15, 1859, leading his portion of
the immigrants, one of those wagons carried the newlywed
Rasmussens.

This seismic shift in my reckoning created a permanent
fault line, causing me to read and reread everything with an
eye toward human error and agenda, including my own. As
I struggled to accept that Karen had traveled alongside Mads
with the better equipped and supplied Robert Neslen Company,
I had to put into perspective what difference it would really
make. Could it alter what Karen and I shared, the headstrong
character that made us each claim agency as a birthright?
Would it make us any more or any less alike? And why not
consider the implications of the Rasmussen daughters' claims?
Might these shadow aunts lead me to what my father and Rhea
never knew (or refused to acknowledge) about Karen's life
with Mads?

Many other questions bubbled to the surface. What on
earth happened to Karen and Mads? That they'd made a
life and family in Utah I could be sure; Mary Catrena and
Grandmother Evelyn were proof of that. But what had my
father really known about the great-grandfather he wouldn't
speak of, and why had he clung so fiercely to the handcart
story? What other evidence had I overlooked? I'd become so
engrossed in this new version of the Rasmussens' journey that I
had to follow it to its conclusion before I pursued anything else.
I returned to the Robert Neslen Company, but focusing this
time on its more privileged members—specifically Neslen's
own wagon train.

Despite obvious advantages, the wagon-train crossings
were marked by tragedies that rivaled those of the handcart
companies. In the ODR account, Mads spoke of his pride and
pleasure to be under the direct command of President Neslen
who headed the entire emigrant group from its beginnings in

Europe and England, although they were anxious at leaving later than the other branches of the company. They traveled with a well-heeled outfit, for many of the travelers had their own wagons and plenty of supplies. Despite their wealth, the wagon-train parties didn't skirt privations. Ironically, it was the glut of possessions that slowed the Robert Neslen Company, causing great discord and catalyzing unforeseen tragedy.

Elders John Taylor and Franklin D. Richards had been sent by Brigham Young from Salt Lake City to check on the Neslen Company's progress. When they caught up with Neslen at Ham's Fork, they found that five wagons in his train had been lost. Many cattle had perished, some from drinking alkaline water, others from exhaustion. And six people had died.

Immigrant Lars Christian Peterson wrote in his autobiography about the dissolution of brotherly love that slowed the Saints' progress. According to Peterson, many blamed the mounting contention on overloaded wagons, which put undue strain on the oxen. As one after another of the cattle gave out, President Neslen called the company together and reminded them of the weight limit they had agreed upon; he also reminded them that they had agreed to share their oxen, should anyone have difficulty with their livestock. But one convert refused to unload his heavy possessions — stoves, furniture, crockery — and forced the exhausted cattle to pull the massive burden through mud until they dropped dead in their traces.

Members of the company were reluctant to lend cattle to someone weighted by his own greed. As feelings of discord heightened, the man tried to harness a wild cow, intending to display the extreme measure to which he'd been driven in the absence of charity. The wild cow broke loose, stampeding the other cattle. Another man, J. C. Warden, was killed in the melee and several others were wounded, including an unnamed woman. Members of the company then openly blamed the man who had valued his material possessions more than his brothers and sisters in the Gospel. The hoarder shouted his intention to drown himself and strode from camp in the direction of the Platte River. Members of the company found him sitting on the bank, full of self-pity and recrimination, gesturing at the Platte, which had shrunk to a silty ditch too shallow to drown anyone. He buried his possessions there in the soft mud, declaring that one day he'd return to retrieve them. According to Lars Peterson, most of those parties unwilling to leave their goods by the wayside did not remain in Zion. He wrote, "[A]fter apostatizing on their arrival in Utah [they] went back to the Midwest [to] make their homes with their own kind of people." This reverse migration is confirmed by historians such as Edith and Jean Matteson, who wrote about the Morrisite Rebellion of roughly five hundred converts who criticized policies of Brigham Young. Some returned to Nebraska, where they joined other disillusioned immigrants, many of them Scandinavian.

One would expect that a wagon train would easily catch up with handcart groups, but the Neslen Company was waylaid by other exigencies: A herd of buffalo took their time grazing in a valley the Saints had to cross, so they waited precious days for the herd to move. A prairie fire delayed them further. One band after another of starving Indians — Sioux, Shoshone, and Ute — stopped them and asked to be fed, saying that the Gold Rushers and other pioneers had ravaged their hunting grounds and stripped berries and other wild forage from the woodlands that had previously provided for them. The *Book of Mormon* taught Latter-day Saints that these Natives were descendants of an ancient tribe of Israel, the Lamanites (named so as the progeny of Laman and Lemuel), which persuaded the Latter-day Saints to be kinder than other white settlers to the Indians. The Saints fed them, shrinking their own supplies. Certainly, some leaders understood that the great tide of LDS immigrants had been among the crowds who stripped the land bare, leaving the Natives homeless and hungry.

After connecting with each company's leaders, Elders Taylor and Richards would eventually conclude that rumors of the immigrants' deprivations had been exaggerated. I wonder how handcart immigrants Sarah Beesley, William Atkin, and Mathias Nielsen would have responded to the Elders had they been given the opportunity.

Latter-day Saints like to claim their families' part in the heroic effort to establish Zion, of which the handcart pioneers' story is quintessential. In a religious culture where martyrdom is the penultimate goal with celestial eternity the reward, icons such as Joseph Smith suggest that personal sacrifice is the price of eternal life, thus encouraging people to spiritualize suffering. In addition, most people seem to shape their ancestral stories to validate their own experience. The progeny of those early members often emphasize their forebears' suffering, especially if they are struggling with deprivation themselves.

My own fundamentalist family carried their identification with martyrs to extremes. We lived in poverty and persecution, so of course we identified greatly with those who paid for their great faith with their fortunes, their health, and their lives. Our Mormon fundamentalist precepts revolved around early doctrines, the Principle of Plural Marriage and the United Order. Living outside the law, without validation from our parent church or the dignity of citizenship, we were left as our ancestors had been, to resist our persecutors, endure our poverty, and hope that God would provide. We were sometimes homeless or on the lam, often frightened, usually marginalized once people learned our polygamous identity. Sometimes we children grew bitter about the imposition of our way of life and we longed to give up the quest and return, but to what? Our trajectory had been cultivated by pioneers who endured similar confusions, exclusions, and abandonment. It was a test of faith, we told ourselves, and we must pass the test or forfeit meaning in this life and eternal glory in the next. And our pioneer ancestors offered the best allegory for the painful contradictions of our lives.

When Robert Neslen's wagon-train company topped Emigration Canyon on September 15, 1859, a crowd of Salt Lake Saints met them. The Neslen Company had prepared a covered cart drawn by a small white ox, wreathed in flowers and displaying a banner: "Hail Columbia, This Beats the Handcart." Given the Neslen Company's considerable difficulties, it couldn't have beat the handcart by much — an irony that may have been obvious to the handcart pioneers who'd preceded them. The Saints of Utah had filed into the canyon and lined the road into Salt Lake City to cheer the immigrants on. They sang hymns and songs of encouragement as the newest group of pioneers made their way into the valley.

The 1859 immigrant company may have expected a cadre of capable Relief Society women to house and clothe them, for their missionaries and company leaders had spoken praises of the good women who welcomed ragged and exhausted immigrants with hot meals and clean clothing, with blankets and shelter. That they came to welcome the Neslen Company and offered what they could indicates the unflagging commitment of Latter-day Saint women to their credo, for Brigham Young had suspended the women's organization in 1844 when Emma Smith used her leverage as Relief Society President to oppose plural marriage and to defy Brigham Young's office as the new President of The Church of Jesus Christ of Latter-day Saints.

In 1859, when Mads and Karen arrived in Zion, the Relief Society had not been officially reconvened, yet the sisters hadn't lost their spirit or sense of purpose. In Utah, Karen would be absorbed into an informal structure formed by women who had not forgotten that "charity never faileth," and who served of their own accord. The women provided large baskets of fresh fruit for the weary immigrants as they arrived at Emigration Square. The travelers deposited their belongings in the public square and were fed hot meals by energetic and kindly women. The choir performed for the immigrant Saints, reminding them with hymns why they had journeyed and suffered to exhaustion.

Residents guided the immigrants to campsites and took from their own stores to help those in need. The immigrants spent their first night in Zion on the ground, but no one seemed to mind. Having a full stomach and being surrounded by kind and watchful brothers and sisters was tantamount to paradise. That may have been the night when Karen vowed to herself that once established in Zion, she would do the same for others in need: provide for the weary travelers and hungry natives, offering shelter to exhausted and lonely souls who materialized on the West's rugged horizon.

Missionaries to Denmark had promised also that Latter-day Saints would shelter those immigrants who had nowhere to winter, and that the Church would help them establish homes and livelihoods. But when the immigrants arrived, they found that the people of Utah were still reeling from their own hardships. Latter-day Saints of Zion were recovering from drought, plagues of "Mormon crickets" (a type of katydid), and the Big Move catalyzed by the Utah War, which had begun two years before Karen's immigration to Zion.

While still in Denmark, Karen had realized that secrecy and persecution were the price she must pay for her new faith. She had dreamed of Zion, where the Saints had gathered to live in peace and harmony. Although she may have known something of the Utah War through whispers that crept abroad when the Perpetual Immigration Fund was dismantled, she couldn't have possibly anticipated the forces that would continue to affect the Mormon faithful in America, even in the Zion she'd endured so much to reach.

For the Saints throughout America, intervention of the federal government in the Church's affairs raised the specter of previous persecutions involving government, particularly the assassinations of Joseph and Hyrum Smith. Some called the US government's escalation of military power in Utah from 1857 through 1858 "Buchanan's Blunder," for it was motivated by political promises to bury slavery and polygamy rather than by a real threat to the United States. Under the governorship of Brigham Young, who had been appointed by James Buchanan's predecessor, Millard Fillmore, polygamy had been practiced widely and openly in Utah since 1852. In 1856, forces under the command of Colonel A. S. Johnston (who was promoted to general in the course of his command) had gone west to quash the rebellion called Bleeding Kansas. Instead of enjoying a hard-earned furlough, Johnston was forced to change plans when President James Buchanan took office. In 1857, mindful of promises to prohibit slavery and polygamy in the territories, Buchanan ordered the soon-to-be-promoted General Johnston to continue westward on a "Utah Expedition." (Interestingly, Johnston fought for the Confederacy in the Civil War and died at Shiloh, the highest-ranking commander on both sides to be killed in battle.)

Just as Karen would have been prepared neither for conflicts between Utah Saints and the US government nor for the Civil War, she wasn't primed for the actual practice of plural marriage. Because polygamy had provoked ire in Denmark, many missionaries avoided speaking of it altogether or, when pressed, spoke of it only as a celestial ideal, not to be lived in this world but in the next.

From 1831, when Joseph Smith first considered plural marriage, until the Saints' arrival at Winter Quarters in the late 1840s, the Latter-Day Saints tried to keep all knowledge of polygamy secret, because of the backlash it generated among non-Mormon fellow citizens. Joseph Smith and his brethren had publicly denied the practice yet privately espoused the celestial blessings of plural marriage. Even while Smith himself and other men in power such as Brigham Young, Heber C. Kimball, and Parley P. Pratt wed handfuls of wives and a growing percentage of the Latter-day Saint population belonged to polygamous households, members denied the actual practice of their sacred doctrine.

Talk of spiritual wives exacerbated the suspicion toward these so-called Saints who touted new scriptures and a living prophet. Mobs tarred and feathered Church leaders and burned barns and homes in Missouri and Illinois. Rumors of spiritual wifery galvanized militias with the task of ridding the country of this peculiar people. One militia-turned-mob grew from Executive Order 44, known as the Extermination Order, signed by Governor Lilburn Boggs on October 27, 1838. The order dictated that Church members be treated as enemies and be driven from the state of Missouri or executed, and a 2,500-man militia was called up to enforce the order. Three days later a Missouri militia raided the Mormon settlement at Haun's Mill, murdering seventeen people, including three boys—ages seven, nine, and ten—which militia members justified under the premise that "nits will make lice." Bodies were mutilated, women raped, and children beaten. The militia slaughtered and stole livestock and burned buildings. No attackers would ever be brought to trial. When the Extermination Order was published, Joseph Smith was in Far West, Missouri, sheltering in the home he had purchased from Edward Partridge, who had purchased it from George Hinkle, a colonel in the Mormon-controlled militia of Caldwell County. Upon Hinkle's urging, Joseph Smith agreed that the Mormon Militia should lay down their arms. When they had done so, the Prophet went out to hear the terms of his surrender, not realizing that Hinkle had already betrayed him.

Encouraged by Hinkle, Major General Samuel D. Lucas of the Missouri militia arrested the Church leaders and convened a tribunal; they sentenced Joseph Smith and four compatriots to execution. Lucas ordered his subordinate, General Alexander W. Doniphan, to carry out the sentence at 9:00 the next morning. My great-great-grandfather William Moore Allred was among those members of the Mormon Militia who lay down their arms and watched in terror as the mob championed Lucas and called for the Prophet's execution. Doniphan, whose fair-mindedness saved the Prophet's life, declared to Lucas, "It is cold-blooded murder. I will not obey your order . . . . If you execute those men, I will hold you responsible before an earthly tribunal, so help me God." Although the 1839 Missouri Legislature hotly debated the legality of the Extermination Order, it was not reversed until June 25, 1976, by Governor Christopher S. Bond. For 137 years, it was legal to kill a Latter-day Saint in Missouri.

When Joseph was housed in the Liberty Jail, Hinkle returned to Far West and ordered Emma and her children to leave the Smith home. He seized the furniture and household goods, as well as Joseph's horse, saddle, and bridle. When Emma took refuge in the home of Lucinda Harris, Hinkle followed and ordered her to leave the area. Apparently, Hinkle believed that Joseph's captors intended to kill the Prophet and that he would be safe in seizing the Smith goods.

Such violence and betrayal fed on rumors of Church-sanctioned polygamy and budding theocracy. The controversy drove the quasi-militia that as a masked mob would attack Joseph Smith and his brother Hyrum in their Carthage, Illinois, jail cell in 1844. Owing to these persecutions, the Latter-day Saint brethren were understandably reluctant to acknowledge the practice of polygamy. From 1846 to 1847, at the encampment in Nebraska known as Winter Quarters, the Saints hunkered down, preparing to endure the cold weather and wait for spring before they crossed the plains. Here, my Allred grandfathers and other Latter-day Saints dropped their dissembling and lived plural marriage openly, even though many members continued to be secretive. After the Latter-day Saints settled in Utah, Church Historian Orson Pratt announced the doctrine of plural marriage during an 1852 Church conference, and word spread around the world, provoking the animosity toward converts in Karen's homeland.

When the Utah Expedition became the Utah War in March 1857, it posed yet another threat to the peculiar Latter-day Saints, another exorbitant price to pay for their religion. They had fled so far west to avoid harassment, yet persecution followed them. (It's not difficult for me to imagine how those early Saints felt. When we left our compound in Salt Lake City under cover of darkness, hoping to escape a raid on polygamists, our family splintered, relocating to different intermountain states. My mother and her twin sister, who wouldn't be separated, took their children to Nevada, where they hoped to stay under the radar. But the authorities noticed us anyway and watched us carefully. Anything—my broken arm, the home birth of a baby, a midnight visit from our itinerant father—could and did prompt investigation. Sometimes I wished that my father would just make a stand, shout out the truth, and dare them to upend our family; other times I was terrified that he would. Such was my legacy as a daughter of the Saints.)

After the June 1844 assassination of the Prophet Joseph Smith and another forced emigration, Brigham Young declared that the Latter-day Saints would stand firm in Utah. They had come so far to gather at the foot of the Wasatch Mountains and enjoy what they believed was their birthright from God and their inalienable right under the US Constitution, religious freedom. The encroachment of Johnston's Army sent the Saints into a frenzy of motion: Brigham Young ordered the Big Move, instructing his followers to disperse as assigned. He told residents leaving their homes and farms to employ a scorched-earth defense, leaving behind "not one building, nor one foot of lumber, nor a stick, nor a tree, nor a particle of grass and hay that will burn, left in reach of our enemies." He instructed them to burn forts rather than give their enemies shelter, torch their fields rather than leave provisions for the army.

Upon arriving at the Salt Lake Valley, Brigham Young had sent explorers to the outlands to find promising places for the members to establish themselves. The experience of being driven out etched lasting lessons, and Brigham knew that if the Church didn't gain a significant foothold in the West, the persecutions of the East and Midwest would be repeated. The need to grow, and grow quickly, was underscored by the challenges of pioneering, and polygamy served to amplify the Church's strength and membership. The encroachment of Johnston's Army accelerated his plan: He sent the Saints out like spokes of a wheel. Indeed, I have ancestors traversing every spoke: some to the hills surrounding the Great Salt Desert, some north to the Utah and Idaho sides of Bear Lake, some east to Wyoming, and many of them south, to the rich farmland of the Sanpete Valley to the stunning rock formations that would be known as Zion Canyon and to the red rock mesas of Utah's Dixie.

As usual, women were expected to provide in the absence of their husbands, fathers, brothers, and sons, for many men had gone to the canyons to build and occupy fortresses. When the men answered Brigham Young's calls to arms or to serve as missionaries or to explore the western deserts, the women kept the hearth, but they also planted gardens, sank fence posts, and raised sheep and cattle. They fed and schooled the children. They taught doctrine and led the singing and sometimes presided at religious meetings. They sheared sheep and carded and spun wool, weaving it into cloth to be sold for lumber, seed, and livestock. They engaged in commerce with each other whenever possible, and they couldn't always afford to heed Brother Brigham's warning against trading with "gentiles" — anyone who was not a member of the Church.

The Utah War lasted fourteen months, from May 1857 to July 1858, disrupting the quietude of the Saints and hovering over the mountains and canyons of the Wasatch Front like a storm cloud about to burst. Under the keen direction of Brigham Young and the remnant of the Nauvoo Legion under the command of Lieutenant General Daniel Wells, Latter-day Saints developed strategies for harassing the federal troops, hoping that they would stand down and go back the way they came. My great-great-grandfather, William Moore Allred, holed up with his brothers and sons (including his little boy, Byron Harvey, who would be my great-grandfather) in Echo Canyon. Byron had already demonstrated his bold spirit at the age of four when his father's family crossed the plains. According to William's autobiography, little Byron fell from the wagon but "lited [sic] on his feet and sprang forward just in time to save himself."

During the Utah War, Byron was ten years old and he helped the men build great bonfires along the canyon walls. Drawing on trickery used during the Revolutionary War, the men and boys delighted in casting monstrous flickering shadows, dashing back and forth before the fires to frighten Johnston's Army with their size and number. They stampeded federal pack animals, set fire to supply trains, and conducted nighttime raids, yelling like marauding Indians, growling like wild animals, anything to keep the US troops from sleeping. They set grassfires to envelop tents and wagons and blocked roads by felling trees and diverting rivers.

When Johnston's Army departed a year later, many families decided they would not return to their abandoned or burned-out homes and began the process of pioneering once again. They established homesteads in Southern Utah and Northern Arizona, built rough cabins, and excavated dugouts. Some moved their children and their belongings to the San Juan Mountains bordering Colorado and the red arches of Moab;

some moved farther north into Idaho; some pressed the edge of the west desert where the Salt Flats stretched for mile after thirsty mile.

After the Big Move, parts of northern Utah were hardly more than ghost settlements. By the time Mads and Karen arrived in the Salt Lake Valley, the Utah War was over, but those already established there had their own challenges to face. Once their welcoming celebration was concluded, the immigrants were left to make their own way. Most camped in Emigration Square and waited for direction. Gradually, they were called into meetings to receive their marching orders from the Brethren, who challenged them to claim homesteads and create lives for themselves. They must put their shoulder to the wheel, as urged in a favorite hymn, just as they had done when they were sunk in the mud of the Great Plains and the snow of the Rockies. It was time for them to establish Zion.

According to family stories, the Rasmussens met with the Lion of the Lord himself, probably in the parlor of the Lion House, located in downtown Salt Lake City. If his meeting with them unfolded as it did with other immigrants, Brigham Young would have welcomed them to Zion, pausing to have his words translated as necessary. Then he would have ordered them to migrate north where they would reclaim the lands abandoned during the Utah War.

The couple did not linger in Salt Lake City long enough for Karen to taste the full power of the Latter-day Saints there. She and Mads would return eight months later to be "sealed for time and all eternity" in the Salt Lake Endowment House by Brigham Young himself. The sealing for time was a material marriage, meaning that they would legally live together as man and wife during their earthly dispensation. The sealing for eternity signified that they were sealed to each other in marriage forever, with their prospective children also sealed to them. They soon found that in Zion, some were sealed for time and not eternity, and some for eternity but not time. Brigham Young, for instance, was sealed for time to the eternal wives of Joseph Smith so that he might see to their welfare since their husband was no longer on the earth, but he would relinquish them to Joseph Smith in the eternities.

Had she stayed in Salt Lake City Karen might have met some of the *grandes dames* of Zion. How wonderful if she had met Sarah Granger Kimball, hostess of the meeting that spawned the Relief Society, a pioneer who created the enormously beneficial wheat program that allowed the Church to extend charity to a needy world and who started a Mormon cooperative that morphed into America's first department store, zcmi (Zion's Cooperative Mercantile Institution). She might have encountered Zina Diantha Huntington Young, the third president of the Relief Society, who was among a handful of Mormon women who lived in polyandry as well as polygyny, because she remained married to Henry B. Jacobs after she was sealed for eternity to Joseph Smith, and later married to Brigham Young for time, only. Among the women of stature emerged a journalist, speaker, and feminist named Emmeline Wells, who would edit an early women's newspaper (*Woman's Exponent*) and who became personal friends with Susan B. Anthony and Elizabeth Cady Stanton. And Karen might even have met poet laureate Eliza R. Snow, who eventually replaced Joseph Smith's wife, Emma, as the First Lady of Zion. Had Karen associated with these women and felt their influence, might she have been more inclined to leave a written record, something that in her own words would explain what I was struggling to understand?

A class system had already developed among this peculiar people regardless of their beehive behavior. In the 1860s and '70s, as the trials of the Early Days receded, Latter-day Saint women of means exchanged the loose, drab homespun of boxy Deseret garb to fashionably cut dresses of silk and wool. Some women had gone into business for themselves, while others attended the co-educational Deseret University (which would become the University of Utah) and actively participated in shaping the community. The women mounted a huge arts and crafts exhibit to be displayed at the Territorial Fair and later at the 1893 World's Columbian Exposition in Chicago. Had Karen stayed in the Salt Lake Valley, she might have thrived, for she was no ordinary woman. She, alone, had made the decision to join the Church, leave Denmark, and come to Zion. But by the time she had married, crossed the Atlantic and the Great Plains, and met the new Prophet of The Church of Jesus Christ Latter-day Saints, she had put her willful being in the closet and given herself over to obedience.

CHAPTER 3

Building Zion

ACCOUNTABILITY IS an important principle in The Church of Jesus Christ of Latter-day Saints. Children are not baptized until they are eight years old, because all baptized members must agree through baptism to be accountable for their choices and their actions. The first choice before them concerns whether they will partake of Christ's redeeming sacrifice and the guidance of the Holy Spirit. This emphasis on choice urges a mode of progression, encouraging continual intellectual, emotional, physical, and spiritual improvement. I remember when my father, who by now had been excommunicated for living plural marriage, doused me in the frigid water of Flathead Lake, saying the sacred words over my submerged body, and how I rose, gasping, and knowing that the burden of my choices from this point on rested on me. A year later, when I chose to be baptized into the official Church of Jesus Christ of Latter-day Saints by my brother Louis in the chlorinated fount of the Elko Nevada Stake Center, I had begun a formal departure from fundamentalism and had begun to feel the weight of agency. I understood it as a basic tenet of democracy, that each person had a choice, a voice, a vote. It became a terrifying and illuminating presence that lit my days and haunted my nights. Incantations of account-ability throbbed in my blood: "The glory of God is intelligence"; "School thy feelings"; "My body is a temple" shaped the landscape of my life as they had my parents' and grandparents'. And surely, given everything they were facing in Early Zion, it shaped my great-great-grandparents, too.

By the time Karen arrived in Zion in September 1859, she had become an avid student of English. While crossing the Atlantic, she had asked for the English names of things on the ship and continued the practice on the train that took them through Canada and on the riverboat that took them to Florence, Nebraska. Some English speakers probably dreaded her sitting beside them, for fear they would spend the whole meeting interpreting. Others delighted in the opportunity to teach and welcomed her questions. By the time they crossed the Great Plains, Karen could communicate many of her thoughts in English. By the time she arrived in Utah, she had decided that her family would speak no other language.

Although she appreciated her fellow Danes, she gradually developed an abhorrence of the Danish language. The memory of her father's condemnation, and the vile accusations of the towns-people, echoed in her head. Along with her new life, her new husband, and her new homeland, she wanted a new language. Eventually, she would try to impose her distaste for her native tongue on her children, who did as most children do, resisting her rule by developing an avid interest in all things Danish.

But her husband, Mads, was more comfortable with his Danish background and less concerned with cultural progress. The tasks before them—surviving the wilderness, adapting to the customs of a new homeland, and developing a liveli-hood—were challenging enough. As a sailor, Mads could speak a little English, but he was happy to meet others who spoke his mother tongue, despite Karen's disapproval. He was an adventurer on land as well as at sea, crossing rivers and mountains and plains with great joy in discovery. But I imagine that Mads dreaded the moment he would have to stop traveling. Since the day he ran away from home to be a sailor, he had been rising and rolling, pushing forward and pulling backward, jumping across and beyond—momentum was something he could comprehend and put to great use. It was in his blood, a nomad song that wouldn't be stifled.

Even with the Promised Land beneath his feet, I suspect Mads struggled with being expected to sink roots and stay in one place like a tree needing only a bit of water and some sunshine. His daughters wrote about his passion for moving things, of freighting. Of course he loved it: all that riding out with a loaded wagon, forging or floating upon the river, traversing the mountains, leaving one settlement to find another, always carrying necessary and delightful goods that made people smile. I've known that wanderlust. Even after I'd made my wedding vows, my gypsy soul wouldn't stop moving. My work became an excuse to travel throughout the United States and across the ocean to teach people and learn from them. I saw it in my father, who didn't really seem to mind that his practice of plural marriage compelled him to travel from house to house, from state to state—even from nation to nation— to sustain his many families. Wasn't it also in his grandmother, Mary Catrena, who left her children, day or night, to attend the sick or deliver a baby, sometimes gone for days at a time?

When, after the Utah War, Brigham Young called select Saints to claim settlements in northern Utah, he urged them to help the Lamanites, by which he meant Shoshone and Ute tribes who hunted and fished in the mountain valleys. Mads would have embraced the move into Indian country. Karen may have objected to so short a stay in civilized centers, but she helped Mads pack their gear and move north to Centerville. Both exercised their agency in obedience.

What they found might have been a root cellar before it became a gambling nook for Johnston's soldiers. Karen and Mads would have descended into the ground like moles, clearing out mud and broken bottles, bits of leather and brass, and lumps of something Karen didn't want to identify. She helped Mads place timbers in the ceiling to shore up a single window and an earthen ceiling soggy with rain and snow. Like other pioneer women, Karen would have made curtains from her tattered petticoats. I know through Aunt Rhea that Karen used the ragged clothing they had worn on their Utah trek to knot a rug for the earthen floor. Together they made a home and got about the business of making a family.

Karen conceived and lost two babies before they'd fully developed, one miscarriage after the other. I know from experience that her heart ached, her mind burned with loss and her body with failure. To complicate things, Mads, the sailor, could not have been entirely happy. I know that the dugout's west-facing window did not reveal when day had dawned. How he must have felt the tyranny of breathing in that hole in the ground. I can see him rushing out to find stars still lighting the eastern sky, stretching to his full six feet and inhaling the sharp air until his lungs ached and his head spun. Wide awake, he must have paced the land, imagining a garden, a house. He would turn and stare out at the shimmering Great Salt Lake, in the moonlight a mirror of the Holy Land's Dead Sea, fed by its own Jordan River. People would have told him that the Salt Lake was so shallow and salty nothing lived there, and no one could possibly drown in it — but how his heart must have yearned for a boat and some sails to trim on the pale horizon set by a semicircle of gray-blue mountains.

The Rasmussens had fully settled into the Centerville dugout when they discovered that Karen was pregnant a third and promising time. Mads's yearning for the sea might have been tempered by the prospect of fatherhood; he would plant

his huge garden and fields of wheat as his father had done in
Denmark. He may have written home to ask for money to buy
livestock and tools. (By then he would have corresponded regularly with his father and mother, encouraging them emigrate,
urging them to study Church scriptures, and to become members as soon as possible.) Mads needed a plow and a strong team
of oxen. Karen would need a cow and a goat to make cheese
and butter. She would need looser clothing. For now, Mads
could shore up the walls of the dugout and level the earthen
stairs with planks from the lumber mill; he could carry car-
rots and beets and shriveled apples from the bishop's storehouse
in Salt Lake City so that Karen would have fresh food. But
Karen, besieged with morning sickness, could choke down
only a little broth, no more. True winter came on, harsh and
cold. Even the enclosure of the ground embracing them could
not keep Karen warm. It was a foreign cold — not the bright
singing cold of the fjords and highlands but the deep dry cold
of an ancient sea gone to salt flats. Surely Mads went hunting
and left Karen shivering on the straw mattress, wearing every
petticoat, dress, and pair of stockings she owned, plus her coat,
hat, and mittens. I imagine that he returned with a little meat
and with the stinking skin of a wolf or a coyote, and she would
throw up before she could thank her husband, wrap herself in
the fur, and sleep.

They named the baby Laura. From the day she was born
in early spring, she was weak and limp, her face like a waxen
doll's. She slept and slept, until Karen flipped her fingers at the
soles of the perfect little feet, trying to wake her to eat. Baby
Laura was slow to nurse and seemed to lack the energy to draw
enough nourishment from the nipple. Floppy as a kitten, every
day she slipped farther away from them and into that other
place. Karen learned to milk her own breasts and to soak a
clean knot of cloth in the saucer of breast milk, then drip it into
the tiny circle of the baby's mouth. Despite her parents' best

efforts, holding her between them at night to keep her warm, coaxing her to stay and praying over her, Laura lived only one month. Brother Porter and other men from the ward came and gave everyone blessings. They said that the baby had acquired the mortal body she had come to claim, and that she would be theirs for all eternity.

Karen, like other mothers who have, in losing their babies, lost pieces of themselves, tried to fathom it. How could this cold little doll be alive anywhere but in her heart? Karen did not cry, silent as her baby, as if the two had made a pact to accept the tragedy of her brief life in stoic silence. After the brethren, the sisters came. They bustled down the new steps to the earthen floor and spoke praises of the curtains and the rag carpet and the coverlet on the straw mattress. They brought what they had, fresh cheese and bread and raspberry preserves. They washed and anointed Laura's tiny body and dressed her for burial. Then the women washed and anointed Karen's body and promised her she would bear a child again, and soon. The ground had thawed and the flowers had begun to bloom the May morning Mads and Karen put their firstborn in the ground. The grieving mother wanted to climb into the grave with her tiny waxen doll, pull earth as a coverlet over the two of them, and sleep forever.

But Karen was made to survive heartache. The lovely aspects of faith—the serenity and resilience of knowing that all things are part of the grand design—may have eluded Karen for a time as she struggled to accept the loss of her baby. But she was not lacking in perseverance. She moved diligently through the day, sweeping the earthen floor until it shone like hard stone, just as my father's wives would do in the deserts of Mexico, where they had gone to live the Principle of Plural Marriage without interference from the US government, and as my mother and her twin sister would do when we hid from the law in an abandoned mining camp, ten of us living among the black lava hills in a dirt-floored, one-room tin shack. Like my mother, Karen washed and hung fresh curtains at the single window to make something civilized in the wilderness. Once a week she scrubbed clothing in water collected from the stream and heated over an outdoor fire, hanging it on sagebrush to dry in the bright, sharp air. She went on forays to collect berries and vegetables. Once a month she pulled everything outside to sweep dust and spiderwebs away. Karen took comfort in these daily tasks just as my mothers and grandmothers did, believing that if by turning her "hands to work and heart to God," her spirits would improve.

Karen remembered the sisters' reassurance that she would bear another child, and she struggled to believe that God would give her a baby to quell the yearning that her brief time with Laura had awakened. After a year of dutiful activity, Karen knew that the sisters' promise held true, for she had conceived again. The dugout had expanded onto a patio of gray river rocks surrounded by gardens and young orchards. Young Peter (Karen insisted on the English spelling of his father's middle name) was a lusty, happy child, and his father adored him. Karen would stand on the porch holding her baby, pointing as his father walked the land, cultivating rows of beets and corn, threshing the golden circle of wheat, stopping now and then to gaze at the Great Salt Lake. I know how fraught such moments are: Karen must have thought her heart would break with fear and joy. How long could this new happiness last?

In the next two years, the brethren in Salt Lake City would have called Mads to come for a meeting. It's not hard to imagine Karen's dread. She couldn't be sure what the brethren would ask of them but, as with most Latter-day Saint women who waited to see why their husbands had been called by the brethren, she feared it would take him away from her, on a mission to Denmark, or to settle some wilderness somewhere, or — heaven forbid — to take a new wife. Devout Saints who were also good providers were more likely to be called to live plural marriage. I know how her heart must have clenched as she waited to hear about the disposition of their lives.

I can see Mads riding up to the dugout door and Karen waiting there, anxious for his news. Did he shout it out or, anticipating her objections, murmur or mumble the plans he'd made with the brethren to move his little family into Weber Canyon? When she learned of the move, perhaps Karen forgot herself and spoke in Danish. But Mads's love of adventure must have infused his face and body; he told her that they would live near a place called Richville. At first, Karen could not fathom why he would leave the comfortable home they had worked so hard to establish, along with their crops and orchard and their friends in the Centerville Ward. How long did it take her to realize that his sailor's heart would always long for new horizons?

She must have recognized that arguing about it would launch a battle she would lose. Morgan County was what Mads wanted and what the brethren wanted for him. Karen may have comforted herself, surmising that in the mountain community called Richville, Mads would build her a real house where they could raise their children and live out their days together.

Her strong sense of ownership would have prompted her to ask: "Will we keep this land?" She gestured to the little plot of ground where Baby Laura was buried as a reminder of how precious it was.

"No, *kaereste*," he would have said, all tenderness in knowing that leaving the grave would be the hardest part of moving.

Karen would have felt, in the grief of moving from Centerville — just as she had when she was cast out of her home in Denmark — the weight of her choice to become a Latter-day Saint. But her agency was the birthright on which she had staked her membership in the Church and her immigration to Zion; once committed, a great many choices pertaining to her life would be foregone, made by others. I imagine her packing their belongings with tears in her eyes, cleaning every mote from the dugout, and making a solitary pilgrimage to the tiny grave. By the time she climbed into the wagon and settled beside Mads, lodging one-year-old Peter on her lap, she resolved to be happy in a new place, just as she had when leaving her father's home in Denmark and later, when stepping aboard the steamship at Copenhagen. The team of oxen took them north and east for twenty miles up Weber Canyon, where the willows grew thick along the Weber, a river so swift and cold that Karen trembled with thoughts of what would happen to her tender little boy if he should fall into the tumble of snowmelt gone mad.

If there is reliable knowledge contained in the bloodline, I've no doubt that she tempered her anxiety into snappish excitement; she would have fussed over Peter's dirt-smudged face and brushed at spots on her husband's dark suit as they drove the carriage through sagebrush past the sparse hamlets of Weber Canyon. They encountered vestiges of the Utah War and Brigham Young's torched-earth policy—burned fields gradually reclaimed by weeds, abandoned homes and farms in disrepair or altogether ruined. Of those houses left standing, many had been occupied by soldiers of Johnston's Army, who had torn apart barns and fences for firewood, stabled their horses in parlors, and penned chickens and pigs in kitchens. Some of the original residents had never returned, preferring milder temperatures in Southern Utah. Mads and Karen had been assigned to one of the abandoned properties. Here they would build yet another dugout, a home Mads would carve from a hillside.

With her Nordic roots, Karen found herself very much at home in chilly Weber Canyon, where the winter sun reached her doorstep only a few hours a day. She soon learned that they lived in what had been Shoshone Territory, and that many of the natives lingered, poor and starving, frequently asking for something from the white people who had settled on their hunting grounds. Karen remembered her own homeless days in Denmark, how she relied on the kindness of Latter-day Saints. True to the direction given by Brigham Young that the Saints should help impoverished natives, she gave the Shoshone what she could. (Her daughters, particularly Mary Catrena, would emulate her generosity with Native Americans, feeding them and attending their births whenever requested.)

On sunny days, Karen rolled up her sleeves, tied a tether from Peter's waist to her own, and set to work alongside her husband. Coming from hardy stock, she didn't complain about having to plow and plant fields, although she might have objected to Mads's way of gazing for long minutes at the horizon. She had been well schooled in the labor of farming, as well as the finer things in life.

She brought with her to Zion a heritage of individual rights in addition to a palate for cultivated living. In Salt Lake City, the fine skills Karen's mother had taught her — weaving, embroidery, and painting — would have combined with her substantial public education to make her welcome among those attuned to the national women's movement then blossoming even in the Western territories. Given Mads's claim to noble blood, she might even have held her own among Zion's progressive women.

As a woman in Utah Territory, Karen had the right to own property, run a business, and receive an advanced education. The freedoms Brigham Young had granted women in Utah Territory could have opened doors to learning and prosperity. But her attention and energies were riveted on pioneering Weber Canyon and battening down her landlocked sailor.

Mads and Karen had been exposed by degrees to the Principle of Plural Marriage, but they were so preoccupied with their own survival that I wonder if they worried much about having to live it. It had seemed innocuous enough when they first heard about it, another Latter-day principle to defend when their friends and parents attacked their faith. Only three percent of the men lived it, although they created exponential growth through wives and children. (This may be an onto-logical justification of plural marriage, to shore up the Church against the losses of emigration and pioneering.) Mads and Karen focused on their own prosperity, and it would not dawn on them until later that if they thrived, the brethren would eventually require more of them—more than the move from the growing community of Centerville to war-ravaged Indian Territory, more than contributing excess food to the United Order, more than paying a regular tithe.

In more populated and affluent sectors of Mormon Utah, a plural wife seldom felt the effects of censure; some even found advantages in living the Principle. A plural wife could bear children and still attend college or run a business—provided a sister-wife would assume her share of domestic duties. In rural Utah, attitudes toward plural marriage varied from commu-nity to community. For a time in St. George, monogamous wives were regarded as distinctly inferior and were sometimes excluded from female gatherings. Yet in Weber Canyon, where federal troops had recently billeted, the Saints were more cir-cumspect, if not secretive, about their marital circumstances. The imperative toward concealment makes it more difficult to know the degree to which polygamy was countenanced in Weber Canyon but might also have given Karen and other strong-willed women more certainty in monogamy and more latitude to exercise agency than did their sisters in other rural areas.

Karen was soon absorbed into Richville's Latter-day Saint sisterhood, meeting with the women to quilt and sew as she learned the language and the gospel. No one seemed to judge the Rasmussens' monogamous state, nor did they hold her

Danish accent against her. She joined the sisterhood, happy to teach her habits of good housekeeping: washing and airing bedsheets, sweeping every speck from the floors, painting doorposts with pitch to keep out insects. She would have cross-stitched the Relief Society motto, Charity Never Faileth, and placed it over the hearth to reinforce her daily practice of making blankets for the sick and for new babies born into the community, of delivering bread and vegetables to the needy, of offering a meal to any hungry Shoshone who wandered to her door.

In Salt Lake City, the sisterhood was also engaged in helping others, but as survival became less of an overriding preoccupation, they focused on social progress, particularly on developing capabilities that could transform charity into movements. From the moment Brigham Young ordered his congregation to go west, the people of the Church had moved steadily forward, taking in stride their prophet's assassination, forced emigration, plagues of crickets, and the Utah War. Women went to college and then became founders and proctors of schools such as Brigham Young Academy (which would become Brigham Young University). Sister Saints bought land; they planted, harvested, and then sold their crops; they owned businesses and paid hefty tithes into Church coffers; they built charitable foundations and enlisted their neighbors in expanding civility; they opened hospitals and trained their sisters to be nurses and midwives. On these and other foundations, the sisterhood set about building a community that would reflect the kingdom of God on Earth. Such breadth of female freedom in a patriarchal, hierarchical, theocratic culture provokes perplexity and curiosity. To understand the context for flowering agency among the sisterhood, we must look at the early church under Joseph Smith's influence, particularly at those women born into the freedoms budding in post-revolutionary America, especially in states where religious movements accompanied the Second Great Awakening with its revivalism and emphasis on individual divine connection.

As I researched my pioneer grandmothers, I was fascinated to learn that certain strong-minded Latter-day Saint women compared favorably with their peers in other American circles. It was surprising, given that such expansive and liberated attitudes did not characterize most Latter-day Saint women of my grandmothers', mothers', and my own generation. Throughout most of the twentieth century, Latter-day Saint women were encouraged to be meek and pious. And many typically were, especially in fundamentalist populations. Yet among them were those willful women determined to claim their agency, who took flights of imagination, fostered new ideas, and voiced strong opinions. They knew their own minds and bodies. They were considered disruptive and dangerous. I know, because I have been one.

Agency is a tricky thing, often double-edged. The responsibilities associated with agency can advance honor and render growth but can also initiate suffering and sacrifice. When Latter-day Saint founders Joseph Smith and Brigham Young allowed that women were endowed with purposes that extend beyond the earth and into eternity, beyond the home and into the community, many early Mormon women seized the opportunity to develop their own capacities and those of their sisters. In embracing the Restored Gospel against the wishes of her father, Karen initialized such growth and pain for herself. In exercising choice regarding the character of her marriage, she invoked unforeseen consequences that, ironically, would narrow rather than expand her choices. She was in good company, although I doubt that she fully realized this.

Had she become fully acquainted with poet laureate Eliza R. Snow, Grandmother Karen would have identified with her deliberate exercise of agency. Eliza Roxcy Snow had always defied the female stereotype. Born in Massachusetts in 1804, she spent her early years not far from the metaphysical fires that would ignite Emerson, Thoreau, and Alcott. Eliza crafted verse during her early school years, vexing her teachers with her rhyming homework. When her parents moved to Mantua, Ohio, Eliza, age 21, began to publish poetry under the pseudonym of Narcissa. She wrote eulogies for both Thomas Jefferson and John Adams for the *Ohio Star* and the *Western Courier* of Ravenna, Ohio. She ignored opportunities to marry, choosing to remain in her parents' home where she seemed content — much to her friends' dismay — with the serene life of an erudite and eloquent spinster. Her appetite for pure thought and well-wrought words shaped a rich intellectual life and a craving for private spiritual experience reminiscent of Emily Dickinson's.

Eliza R. Snow met Joseph Smith in 1831 through the confluence of geography, persecution, and missionary work. But many years of miraculous events preceded the meeting between the Prophet and the Snow family in Ohio. Joseph Smith had grown up in the area of central and western New York dubbed the Burned-over District because of the intensity and frequency of revival meetings and religious propagation. His family had been caught up in revivalism and attended many churches and heard many philosophies. There, near Palmyra, fourteen-year-old Joseph knelt in a grove and had his first vision of God the Father and Jesus Christ. Smith would relate that subsequent visits from an angel named Moroni directed him to Hill Cumorah, where he excavated the golden plates of Mormon. After translating these ancient plates into English, Smith went to Fayette in 1830 to organize the Restored Gospel of Jesus Christ, which would become The Church of Jesus Christ of Latter-day Saints.

Less than a year later, Joseph and Emma Smith left Fayette for Hiram, Ohio — owing, Joseph would say, to a revelation. In late 1831, Joseph Smith visited the Snow farm in nearby Mantua.

His visit would change everything for Eliza and her family. Owing to his influence, she would trade the serenity of her solitary life for persecution, forced emigration, and eventually plural marriage. She would become a western pioneer and a religious leader. Her brother Lorenzo, baptized in 1836, would one day be imprisoned for polygamy in a jail cell that would later be occupied by my father for the same offense. Besides being an early convert and, as my fundamentalist family likes to say, "a convict for the Lord," Lorenzo would also hold the highest religious office available to him, becoming the fifth president of the Church.

Prior to these developments, Eliza was a thoughtful and cautious woman, and thus she took a careful approach to this new religion Joseph Smith held out to her family. Eliza's mother and sister were baptized soon after they met Joseph Smith, but Eliza deliberated four more years before she, too, entered baptismal waters at the age of thirty-one. Once baptized, Eliza exercised her commitment unreservedly. In December 1835, she followed the Saints to Kirtland, Ohio, where she donated her large inheritance toward the building of the Church's Kirtland Temple. In return, she received a lot with a large house where she taught school to the Smith children. Eventually, Eliza moved in with the Smith family to be the children's governess and she began donating the money allocated for her living expenses to the temple fund.

During her tenure as the Smith children's governess, Eliza wrote two shining songs for the hymnal Emma Smith had been called to compile. She would pen some of the best-loved Latter-day Saint hymns, including an affirmation of female deity, a Mother in Heaven. In the primarily patriarchal culture of America, Eliza had been touched by restorationists intent on the pure teachings of Christ and transcendentalists who believed in the inherent goodness of all people, including women. As she studied the Restored Gospel of Jesus Christ, she sought knowledge about a female deity, an eternal woman the sisterhood could emulate, and she took her questions to Joseph Smith. He reassured her that a Heavenly Mother stood beside Heavenly Father in the eternities. One of her best-loved hymns, "O My Father" (originally titled "Invocation, or the Eternal Father and Mother") declaims:

> In the heavens are parents single?
> No, the thought makes reason stare!
> Truth is reason, truth eternal / Tells me I've a mother there.

Essentially lyrical testimony, this and others of Eliza's hymns have been treasured by Saints as nearly scriptural in scope and influence.

By most markers, however, Mormonism remained entrenched in patriarchy. As in most other churches, women and men did not sit together in those early meetings. For a brief time, Joseph Smith himself conferred upon a few women the titles of high priestess and prophetess. But as usually happens in religious movements, the Church settled into familiar patterns: Men were endowed with the priesthood, while wives could exercise priesthood only through their husbands' authority, usually when no man was available to confer the blessing or ordinance.

Yet Eliza saw in the new church a surprisingly liberal, even revolutionary, window of opportunity for women. She had come to maturity in an era when industrialization and public education had catalyzed dramatic changes. Women across the nation had begun to redefine themselves. The problems posed by industrial and urban populations brought ladies of refinement together to find charitable and cultural solutions to poverty, alcoholism, and poor working conditions. Ladies' Aid Societies became a popular means of promoting culture and pushing back incivility, whether in urban ghettos or on the untamed frontier. This social consciousness infused these early

Latter-day Saint women with a great yearning to perform charitable service, an attitude amplified by the construction of the Nauvoo Temple.

Sarah Granger Kimball, who joined the Church as a teenager, wanted to contribute to the Nauvoo temple, but as her husband was not yet a member of the Church, she felt she could not ask him for money. She conferred with her seamstress, Margaret Cook, and the two decided to gather a group of women together to repair the clothing of the men building the Nauvoo Temple. Kimball hosted the first meeting of this ladies' society in her home and asked the erudite Eliza R. Snow to take notes. As their meeting progressed, the women discussed the purpose of their association, and Kimball asked Snow to draw up a constitution and bylaws. When Eliza R. Snow took the document to Joseph Smith for his approval, he declared that it was the best he'd seen, but countered that he had "something better for them than a written Constitution." He promised a divine organization of women "after the pattern of the priesthood." I wonder how Eliza, who always wrote carefully and responsibly and sought inspiration for her words, felt about her constitution being dismissed. Surely, she was a little disappointed.

On March 17, 1842, the women gathered again, this time in the upper room of Joseph's red-brick general store. At this meeting, which became the first formal meeting of the Relief Society (said to be the largest and oldest women's society in the world), Joseph Smith encouraged the sisterhood to adopt "Charity never faileth" from 1 Corinthians 13:8 as their motto. Joseph invested authority and license in them, promising the women, "I now turn the key to you in the name of God, and this Society shall rejoice and knowledge and intelligence shall flow down from this time." The key he gave them was no physical object but the priesthood authority that, according to Latter-day Saint doctrine, is bestowed on leaders who have proven worthy to exercise the power of God on Earth.

Joseph Smith encouraged the women to elect a president and counselors. Patriarchy, politics, and pecking orders being what they were, it could have surprised no one that the women elected Joseph's wife, Emma, as president. Emma selected her friends Sarah Cleveland and Elizabeth Whitney as her counselors. The minutes of the meeting indicate that Eliza R. Snow was asked to serve as secretary of this first Relief Society.

From her podium as president of the Relief Society, Emma Smith would do great good among the Latter-day Saints. She set an example of Christian charity through her behavior. She initiated service throughout the community and used her authority to alleviate sickness and hunger. Significantly, in 1842 Emma and her sisters organized a petition against abuses of the Mormon people by the state of Illinois and presented it to the governor. Although the petition did little to curtail harassment of the Latter-day Saints, the precedent Emma set by engaging the sisterhood in political activity on behalf of her people set the stage for Latter-day Saint women to pioneer the women's movement by casting their votes in a general election on February 14, 1870.

Emma Smith had also used her Relief Society leadership to lobby against spiritual wifery. She probably believed that her stand against plural marriage was consistent with other ways in which she championed women's value and dignity. Some histories indicate that before she began her crusade, Emma Smith had reluctantly permitted her husband to take spiritual wives, but other accounts insist that she never agreed to polygamy and that as far as she knew, Joseph never consummated a marriage other than her own.

Emma had been loyal to Joseph in myriad ways, marrying him against her parents' advice, supporting his religious inspirations, and navigating domestic difficulties while Joseph was out proselytizing. She managed to visit him regularly during the more than four months he was incarcerated in Missouri's

Liberty Jail. When Missouri Governor Boggs expelled the Saints from the state, she crossed the frozen Mississippi River with four children, scaling the bank at Quincy, Illinois, and settling her family on her own.

Emma was and still is a heroine to Latter-day Saints. Her loyalty to Joseph and to the Gospel had been unswerving. But her aversion to polygamy spawned controversy. Stories circulated: That she'd forced their sixteen-year-old housemaid Fanny Alger to leave the Smith home when she discovered that through a secret ceremony, the girl had become the first of Joseph's plural wives. That she banished her live-in maids, the Partridge sisters Eliza and Emily, when she learned that they, too, were married to Joseph. The possibility that the Prophet had married sisters caught my attention. My mother and her twin were my father's third and fourth wives and I knew that fundamentalist patriarchs recommended the practice of marrying sisters because who better could model the harmony of sisterhood? But I had learned all too well that even between twins, rivalry and comparison could fester into anguish. Often my mother's pain became my own—persistently fanning my desire for agency and monogamy. I knew in my bones that even without Emma's intervention, the Partridge sisters would have been challenged in finding perfect harmony in their marriage to the same man.

Despite the patriarchy's emphasis on sisterhood, Emma was effectually no one's sister, for as the Prophet's first and legal wife, she had no peer. Hailed as the elect lady and consummate example for Latter-day Saint women, Emma may have worked both for and against the patriarchy in her resistance to polygamy. While her loathing may have stirred resistance to the Principle within the Church, it may also have tempered the tumultuous days of persecution, by implying that rumors of plural marriage were unfounded.

For many years, stories surrounded the relationship shared by Joseph Smith, his wife, Emma, and the children's governess,

Eliza R. Snow. As with most members, Eliza's first reaction to the doctrine of plural marriage was revulsion: After her first exposure, she wrote, "[I]t seemed as though all the prejudices of my ancestors for generations past congregated around me." But gradually she embraced plurality as "the fullness of the Gospel in the last dispensation of time," for she'd been taught that all ancient laws must be fulfilled as part of the Restoration of Christ's church in the last days of the earth. Joseph hinted that the Principle would usher in a new and empowered freedom for women. Eliza prepared herself to accept plural marriage—but she regarded it as a challenge awaiting her in some eternal future, certainly not in this material world.

Then Eliza learned that Sarah Cleveland (a dear friend to both Eliza and Emma) had become a spiritual wife to Joseph Smith despite continuing her marriage to her first husband, John Cleveland. As she talked with Sarah, Eliza was thunderstruck with the realization that polygamy was being practiced at that very moment on this earth. She prayerfully set her heartache aside and fortified herself against doubt, preparing to move in the direction her religious leaders commanded. When Joseph asked her, too, to become his wife, she must have felt that eternity had arrived at her doorstep. On June 29, 1842, at the age of 38, Eliza married Joseph Smith, in whom she invested enormous trust and admiration—and managed to find meaning and beauty in this strange way of life.

The change in Eliza's status reverberated through the Smith household, although it seems that no one spoke of it. Everyone in the house would have tiptoed around Emma, whose opinion about polygamy was anything but secret. It takes little for me to imagine the covert culture this must have fostered—the hushed exchanges, the stealthy maneuverings, even outright duplicity. Could it have been so different from the secrecy and dissembling Karen and other Latter-day Saint converts had to practice in Denmark? Or from how my family had to hide our meetings and lie to neighbors and school authorities? Or from the innuendo my plural mothers relied on in referring to their private time with their shared husband? I know about the costs of subterfuge, how family members turn their distrust on each other and on themselves.

Despite mounting tensions, Eliza continued to live with the Smiths. Joseph and Emma's children loved both their mother and their governess and were anxious for the women to live together harmoniously. According to one tale, Emma discovered that Eliza was expecting Joseph's child and flew into a jealous rage; one account suggests that Emma threw Eliza down the stairs, causing miscarriage and permanent damage to Eliza's hip. It's true that Eliza walked with a limp and never did bear children, but no testament that she was pregnant at the time or even that she fell emerges from Eliza's diaries. Biographers of both Emma Smith and Eliza R. Snow discount this story, saying that no reliable record validates these accounts. Only a brief note confirms the change in Eliza's living circumstances with an entry in her diary on February 11, 1843, stating that she had moved her things to the household of Jonathan Holmes.

A 2016 *Salt Lake Tribune* story by journalist Peggy Fletcher Stack counters the rumor that Emma had any part in Eliza's childless state. Stack's story draws from the recently discovered autobiography of Alice Merrill Horne (who founded in Utah the first state arts organization in the United States). Horne remembers a time in the 1880s overhearing as her grandmother, fourth Relief Society president Bathsheba Smith, whispered with the most important women of Mormondom about the Missouri persecutions of 1838 when eight mobsters had gang-raped Eliza. According to Horne's reminiscence, Bathsheba and her friends agreed that this brutal event had introduced Eliza's lifelong limp and probably rendered her incapable of bearing children. Horne's account led historian Andrea Radke-Moss to suggest that Eliza's ordeal moved Joseph Smith to marry her "as a way of promising . . . that she would be a mother in Zion." If Horne's memory is correct, Eliza had tried to conceive. It also confirms that, as she later confided in her stake president Angus Cannon, her relationship with Joseph Smith did have a conjugal dimension.

Regardless of what smoldered at the center of Emma's and Eliza's relationship, the two, who began their relationship with respect and affection, remained scrupulous in their sisterhood. During this stressful time, both women continued in their roles as Relief Society leaders, Emma as president and Eliza as secretary. They had committed themselves to an organization devoted to doing good works, to sharing their time and substance, and to lifting each other up, so that, in the words of Joseph's mother, Lucy Mack Smith, "we may all sit down in heaven together." But Emma Smith's version of sisterhood did not include sharing her husband and household in the material world. Emma contended — in keeping with Eliza's initial impression of the Principle — that Joseph never intended to consummate plural marriages, that they were for eternity only, and not meant to be practiced in earthly ways. Regardless of their private feelings toward one another, the two women soldiered on together within the structure of the Church, firmly entrenched in the service of God and their fellow beings.

The question of whether Joseph Smith consummated plural marriages has risen again and again, particularly with concern for children of women who were already married. In later years, a few women, notably Emily Partridge, Lucy Walker, and Malissa Lott, indicated that they had indeed consummated their marriages to Joseph, and sixteen plural wives were rumored to have had a child by him. Yet not one of these children was presented as Joseph Smith's descendant in Utah when polygamy was lived openly. In 2010, geneticist Ugo A. Perego undertook the exploration of Joseph Smith's line. He tested the DNA of people descending from alleged children of Joseph Smith against the DNA of those descending from his children with Emma. No match resulted, but four of the alleged offspring were genetically traced to the legal husbands of their mothers. Two of these were John Reed Hancock and Orson Henry Hyde, whom Fawn M. Brodie had posited as Smith's descendants in her acclaimed 1945 scholarly biography *No Man Knows My History*. As Joseph was fertile enough to father eleven children with Emma, it seems inconceivable that he would not have fathered at least one child among the thirty-three or more women ascribed to him as plural wives. Perhaps he did hold those plural marriages for eternity only.

Regardless of how Joseph Smith lived his plural marriages, it could not have been easy on him. I can believe that his proposal to Eliza sprang from a deep compassion for what she'd been through, and I can believe that Joseph Smith was deeply committed to the Principle and to each of his wives. You see, my father was just such a compassionate and committed man.

A reluctant spiritual leader born to a plural wife in Mexico but reared in monogamy in the US after his father's first wife died, my father, Dr. Rulon Clark Allred, returned to his fundamentalist roots only after much inner torment and prayer. It cost him his first wife and his membership in his beloved Church of Jesus Christ of Latter-day Saints. Thereafter every commitment, each the result of exhaustive soul-searching, would cost him heavily. He paid. His wives paid. His children paid. But nothing altered who he was, or that we loved him. As a doctor to so many who couldn't otherwise seek medical care, he shared his expertise like so many lifelines. As a reluctant spiritual leader, he bore the weight of thousands who came to him with economic and emotional problems he'd never been trained to solve — not least of which sprang from the legal labyrinths of our outlawed way of life. That he felt his wives' pain — all our pain—I'm absolutely sure. Ultimately, his engagement in the Principle of Plural Marriage would cost him his life. I think about the ironies of his way of life, especially that a man committed to so many could still be lonely. But my father was lonely. No one could really understand what it was like to be him.

From age three I knew that I never wanted to share a husband. By my teens, I saw clearly that our way of life had catalyzed my mother's nervous breakdowns and had generated paucity and spite in otherwise generous and kind people. I also realized that only a person who felt a compelling spiritual call should try to live the Principle; anyone else would make a hell of a mess. I did not feel called to live it. For me, the Principle of Plural Marriage presented a quandary: I owed my life to it, and was grateful for my parents' conviction, but I was tormented by every thought of living it myself.

It took me years to see my father's loneliness and pain for what they were, to grasp what he felt when he swore that he would go to hell, if need be, to reclaim his first wife in the eternities. And having come to understand that, I can imagine what Joseph Smith felt when Emma's heartbreak came between them while the world and even his own brethren raged against him. I can see also how public outcry exacerbated the tempests in his private life. Joseph was under heavy fire from other Americans, especially religious leaders who voiced concerns about aspects of his theology, including his foundational claim to have met Heavenly Father and His Son Jesus Christ in person. Pundits objected strenuously to his introduction of new scriptures, particularly his translation of the golden plates, called the *Book of Mormon*. This claim to new scripture provided an excuse for many to ignore their common ground as believers in the Bible and in Jesus Christ. Politicians fretted about the Mormon bloc of votes, surmising that Church members would vote as their leaders dictated, a phenomenon that could decide the slavery issue and determine who was in power from one county and one state to the next.

But the rumors of polygamy struck a nerve that roused the countryside against the Saints. Tensions about polygamy escalated in 1842, when a confederate of Joseph Smith, physician and Nauvoo mayor John C. Bennett, tried to seduce a young woman, saying that he intended to marry her. Both Mormons and non-Mormons came forward with additional allegations of Bennett's philandering. When confronted by Nauvoo citizenry, Dr. Bennett justified his polygamous behavior, claiming that Joseph, too, practiced spiritual wifery. Spiritual wifery was generally understood to be a thin excuse to indulge in sexual activity, unlike Joseph Smith's teaching about plural marriage, which was meant to be an eternal union confirmed by the power of God. As allegations of adultery proliferated, Joseph Smith dispatched his brother Hyrum Smith and his second counselor in the Church, William Law, to investigate. Smith and Law reported that Bennett's wife had left him over his adultery. One of her friends had told them that Mrs. Bennett "could no longer live with him [as] it would be the seventh family he had parted during their union."

When cornered by Joseph Smith, Bennett confessed that he had used his trusted position as a doctor and a colleague of Smith to seduce women. Emma Smith's nephew, Lorenzo D. Wasson, claimed to have overheard Joseph excoriating Bennett for committing sins through pretended ecclesiastical authority. In a grand display of remorse, Bennett took poison; not surprisingly, he recovered. He provided an affidavit declaring that Smith had no part in his crimes, but the scandal roiled on until Church priesthood leaders charged Bennett with adultery; he was summarily excommunicated from the Church and removed as mayor. Soon afterward, the disaffected Bennett published an exposé of Mormonism and Joseph Smith. Among the stories he exaggerated or invented was that Smith had threatened the life of Missouri governor Lilburn Boggs. The accusations of treason, murder, prostitution, and adultery inflamed American pundits. Although the book was generally deemed more lies than truth, it infected the nation with a view of the early Church of Jesus Christ of Latter-day Saints as a hotbed of promiscuity, outraging Christians everywhere. The spiritual-wifery outcry increased persecution and sullied the Latter-day Saint reputation; polygamy became synonymous with slavery in the public imagination, evoking abolition-ist fervor. Emma Smith had never trusted the man and often referred to the Bennett scandal and his scurrilous behavior in her effort to distance Joseph from polygamy.

Yet some sources indicate that Joseph may have taken his first plural wife, Fanny Alger, as early as 1833, with a hiatus of about ten years before he took others. Early leaders tried to keep the Church's doctrine of plural marriage secret even from the main body of the Church. Consequently, most members of the Church were confused and helpless before the general moral outrage. It would be many years, after the Latter-day Saint body had emigrated west, before the Church countered the widespread accusations of debauchery with a doctrinal defense of religious principle. Meanwhile, Church leaders endured criticism and indictment with unflagging piety.

Despite doctrines regarding the Principle and a vague belief that plural marriage was the only way to attain celes-tial glory — and even though the Brethren took care to pres-ent it as an ancient form of marriage, ordained by God — men and women reared in the monogamy of Protestant homes were repelled by polygamy. The Christian ethos affirming the worth of every soul didn't align well with pluralistic values, where the good of all supplanted individual development. And although Abraham, Isaac, and Jacob had practiced polygamy, the Latter-day Saints' own scripture, the *Book of Mormon*'s "Book of Jacob," decried the practice of having many wives as sinful unless commanded by God. As with the Lutherans of Denmark, converts from Protestant and Anglican faiths had great difficulty embracing plural marriage. Imagine how it was for them, after lifetime training to be chaste and then faithful to a single spouse, to be instructed in this new harmony known as the Most Holy Principle. But Joseph Smith and Brigham Young privately promised their followers that plural marriage would ensure an exalted life. Celestial or Plural Marriage, they said, was a law of God, superior to the laws of men. Because the Lord had commanded it, He would broach no dissent from men, women, or children, Mormon or gentile.

Once plural marriage had been established as the standard of exaltation, first wives were generally inclined to accept it. However, some women asked for and received divorces from husbands who intended to live the Principle, and some men refused to take a second wife, rather than lose the love of their first-wed. Most Mormon men who lived polygamy had no more than two wives. Much of the Latter-day Saint population was not touched by plural marriage. But those women who felt compelled to live polygamy against their wishes were in a quandary. Unlike the betrayed wife who discovers that her husband is involved with the other woman, first wives could not fight polygamy with public censure or moral indignation. Their nemeses were their beloved prophet and their own faith. They found that jealousy was not considered a viable argument against religious mandate, and anyone who sympathized with dissenters was accused of having a weak or false testimony. Seeds of discontent among the Saints were quickly plowed under with other hurts and losses in the name of unity. So long as the Church was hounded and mobbed by outsiders, any sort of internal discord seemed selfish and disloyal.

Few Church leaders refused to jump on the plural marriage bandwagon. Those who stood openly against the Principle reaped consequences. Some of Joseph's staunch supporters were excommunicated for either objecting to polygamy or criticiz-ing Joseph for breaking the code of secrecy by preaching plural marriage to the School of the Prophets, an exclusive gathering of powerful Mormon leaders. Scandalized members had been reassured that the Principle of Plural Marriage was a celestial law, not meant to be lived on earth, and many were placated. Those who believed the rumors spread by Bennett and oth-ers withdrew their membership. Important leaders, including the second counselor to Joseph Smith, William Law, and his brother Wilson, who was a brigadier general in the Nauvoo Legion, left the Church in fury or despair, bitter about the rela-tionships, money, and reputation they'd invested and lost.

Of course, those who stayed paid their dues. Some breth-ren were commanded to give their own wives to Joseph in spiritual marriage, a test of faith that plunged more than one disciple into angst and some into full-scale rebellion. Their dissent and the outrage of their wives spilled into the sur-rounding communities. Polygamy-related controversies may explain some of the persecution that flared up wherever members settled: Masked mobs imposed a variety of tor-ments, from tarring and feathering to house and barn burn-ings focused especially on Latter-day Saint leaders. Although women were not tarred and feathered, many, like Eliza, were raped. Some perished with their children hidden in root cel-lars and beneath floorboards when the Saints' buildings were set ablaze by the mobs.

Many of the conspirators were people in power, including Illinois governor Thomas Ford. Most politicos who used their influence to interfere with Latter-day Saint commerce were primarily concerned about the Mormon bloc of votes. As the Saints ran out of money and provisions, they were forced to give up their property, thus diminishing their voting influ-ence. Church leaders were vilified in the press, accused of every sort of crime. *Mormonism Unvailed! [sic] Mormonism Exposed!*

Antidote to Mormonism! So screamed the titles of pamphlets passed out on street corners.

In the face of persecution and with their men under siege, Latter-day Saint women turned to each other for reinforcement and comfort. Some women found friendship with their sister-wives, while others relied on their children for companionship and still others on the creative impulse.

As one hymn after another flowed from her pen, Eliza R. Snow demonstrated the vigor of her faith in service and obedience, modeling resilience and steadfastness for the congregation. She found beauty, peace, and refinement in a way of life unbelievers condemned as base and lustful. She wrote in her autobiography, "As I increased in knowledge . . . of Plural Marriage, I grew in love with it and today esteem it as a precious, sacred principle — necessary in the elevation and salvation of the human family — in redeeming woman from the curse, and the world from corruption."

She was not alone in her perception. Other Latter-day Saint women voiced similar testimonies of plural marriage, including Zina D. H. Jacobs Young, Presendia L. H. Buell Kimball, and Marinda Johnson Hyde (all of whom were married to men active in the Church at the time they were sealed to Joseph Smith). But these were privileged, educated women who communicated frequently with the most powerful men in the Church — and enjoyed no small compensation in influence. However, most women drafted into plural marriage discovered that the promised blissfulness of celestial life wasn't to be had in the here and now. Although the gain of many shoulders bearing life's burdens could be convenient and comforting, neglected plural wives found their lives more complicated and, in some ways, more taxing than widowhood as they struggled to survive without the community support bestowed on single or bereft women. Too, the tensions of sharing family resources and a husband amplified natural rivalries. Pecking orders sprang up and, inevitably, the dissonances of haves and have-nots marred this utopian ground.

Like most plural wives, Eliza R. Snow did not have much time, private or otherwise, with her new husband. Yet her diary, in which she calls Joseph "my beloved husband, the choice of my heart and the crown of my life," suggests that Eliza was more content than most in knowing that she had eternity to spend with her husband.

Whatever internecine strife wives and families suffered paled in comparison to what they faced in the larger world. Governor Boggs's Extermination Order had raised persecution to previously unimaginable extremes. The Missouri persecutions touched my Allred ancestors, as well. The pattern of religious discrimination had begun in England, carried to America by one of my father's Quaker ancestors who fled persecutions in England with help from William Penn, sought refuge in Pennsylvania and Virginia, then settled his family in North Carolina, where they prospered and acquired land. As the family expanded, they moved westward to Tennessee, then to Missouri.

The Allred brothers converted to The Church of Jesus Christ after meeting Joseph Smith's brother Hyrum, who held the title of Patriarch of the young church, and the Allred brothers helped establish the Salt River Branch of the Church in Missouri, where they enjoyed the ministrations of the Prophet himself. Upon Joseph Smith's direction, my great-great-great-grandfather Isaac Allred, and his brother James, moved first to Jackson County, then to Clay County, and then to Caldwell County. As members of the Mormon Militia, they were dedicated to preventing another massacre like the one at Haun's Mill. At Far West, after breathlessly witnessing Joseph Smith's narrow escape from immediate execution, my great-great-grandfather William Moore Allred, as a young Mormon militiaman, surrendered his arms and promised to move out of the state, giving up all claims to property in order to save his own and the Prophet's life.

Forced to forfeit their lands and emigrate immediately, they herded their families across the frozen Mississippi River. Once Joseph Smith had been released from the Liberty Jail, the purchase of Commerce, Illinois, allowed Church leaders to establish the town of Nauvoo, and the Saints began building a temple. Great-great-grandfather William drove his team of oxen to a nearby quarry to harvest what he hoped would be the cornerstone of the temple. From his journals, I can see that, as with many early Latter-day Saints, William seemed highly conscious of his part in shaping history. By daybreak, he had leveraged the enormous stone into his ox-drawn wagon and departed the quarry before anyone else had arrived, certain that he'd be the first to reach the site where the Prophet and others waited to set the cornerstone. To his everlasting disappointment, another man with a team of high-stepping horses trotted past his slow, strong oxen and arrived just ahead of Great-great-grandfather William. Although his would not be the cornerstone, William's stone was also used, and he considered himself blessed to help set the foundations of Zion in the new world.

William and his father, Isaac, labored daily on the temple. They had little to sustain them, having lost all they had in the Missouri rout. But the citizens of Nauvoo fed them and the prospect of building up the kingdom of God on Earth bolstered their faith. Working with stone shredded their garments and left them threadbare as winter approached; thankfully, William and Isaac were among those who benefitted from the efforts of Sarah Granger Kimball and her sister seamstresses as they launched the enduring Relief Society.

Although the temple was under construction, the Latter-day Saint people had found little refuge. The influx of immigrating Missouri Saints intensified tensions in Illinois. As the

Saints' numbers grew, the established politicos felt the threat of an alien constituency. One early indication of their conflicting purposes surfaced when, feeling the power of their numbers, the Latter-day Saints declared that they wanted Nauvoo to be an alcohol-free town, one that didn't attract gentiles who would get drunk and make trouble. William was working on the temple one day in 1840 when a group of Mormon men decided to shut down the local saloon. William writes of the men who appointed him to stand guard while they intercepted a wagon loaded with spirits and tipped it over a ravine. Repercussions of their vandalism were not recorded in his journal, but the tensions between gentiles and Saints grew palpably and spawned increasing violence.

In Nauvoo, William joined the choir and there he met his bride-to-be, Orissa Angelica Bates. He took note in his journal: "We were married on January 2nd of 1842 by Dr. John C. Bennett. The Prophet Joseph and his wife were present." This marriage took place scant months before Bennett's fall from grace, marking an inauspicious beginning for this devout Latter-day Saint couple. Later, when the Nauvoo Temple was sufficiently finished, William and Orissa received their endowments, consisting of various eternal promises between themselves and God; then the couple was sealed for eternity at the altar in a ceremony conducted by the widely respected Heber C. Kimball, one of the Church's twelve apostles. I imagine that William and Orissa were comforted that their sealing was officiated by someone whose reputation was not in question. The auspicious sealing could be measured by the result: that thirteen of their children reached adulthood and lived prosperous, saintly lives.

Life in Nauvoo was difficult. William and Isaac had left their assets in Missouri and had few resources with which to begin their new lives in Illinois. William complained about the exorbitant amount he paid for a small plot of land on which to build his newlywed home: "I paid $150.00 for a small lot and built a small brick house on it, and then only got $35 for it when we had to leave Nauvoo." His hardship reflects some of the lesser losses borne by the Saints, who invested what little they had in the township they believed would be Zion in the new world.

In addition to William's economic woes, he struggled with health issues. William writes of recurrent bouts of ague — probably malaria. Autumn and winter were bitterly cold for their inadequate shelter, making William's illness worse. The couple's first son was born while William was in the throes of chills and fever: "I was so very sick I couldn't get up. The child came near dying[;] they said he would lay for 15 minutes like he was dead. My wife wasn't very smart and not realizing the consequences she done her washing when the child was one week old, she took cold, and it settled in her breast. Father [Isaac] came and wanted us to go to his house to live, so we went, and she had the worse broken breast I ever saw." Too sick himself to tend his wife, he records further, "I have heard father tell people about it, and he said it was as big as an iron teakettle and nearly as black."

Then a vindictive and outraged presence coalesced from the rumors of spiritual wifery and accusations of sexual misconduct by Church leaders, perpetuated by both disgruntled Mormons and non-Mormons. As the American press stepped up its vilification of all things Mormon, a home-grown newspaper called the *Nauvoo Expositor* jumped on the bandwagon, printing its first and only edition, which stated: "We are earnestly seeking to explode the vicious principles of Joseph Smith, and those who practice the same abominations and whoredoms; which we verily know are not accordant and consonant with the principles of Jesus Christ." This newspaper would pierce

Joseph Smith's heart like no other, for many of the contribu-
tors were former friends and counselors. It seems he turned to
the women — that group he had promised greater freedom and
dignity — for consolation and solutions.

Although friends turned against him and state and federal
agents joined the mounting efforts to stop him, Joseph Smith
did not lose focus on the work of the temple. Nor did he give
up reassuring women of the Church that polygamy was essential to restoring all God's laws. As scholar Lola Van Wagenen
points out, at various times and in various ways, Joseph Smith
promised women "equality and privileges greater than they had
ever known," for "women participated in church governance
through 'religious franchise,' the church's method of voting."

Plural marriage did free women who were educated or
inclined by training or necessity to loosen the bonds of homemaking and move toward their aptitudes. Although most
inclined to hearth and children, others became involved in
community and church work, relying on their sister-wives to
cover the home front. Latter-day Saint women were permitted to vote on church matters along with the men. Latter-day
Saint women were credited with spiritual gifts and endowed
with responsibility for performing ordinances in the beautiful
temple in Nauvoo; they led the congregation in prayer and
were empowered as teachers of the gospel.

Through the prosperity of the Relief Society, the sisterhood
had realized their ability to organize and respond as needed. In
1842, more than a thousand Latter-day Saint women, residents
of Nauvoo and the surrounding area, rallied to sign a petition that Emma Smith presented to Illinois governor Thomas
Carlin. Protesting unjust treatment of Latter-day Saints, the
petition focused most specifically on the impending extradition of their prophet back to Missouri, where Governor Boggs
was maintaining that Smith had tried to assassinate him.
Although Smith had not been in Missouri when the attempt

occurred, Governor Carlin had Smith arrested. However, he also accepted the women's petition. In court, Smith's attorneys addressed Judge Pope, who found himself surrounded by Relief Society sisters and other women — notably including young Mary Lincoln — and succeeded in blocking extradition. Afterward, Smith attended a Relief Society meeting to thank the sisterhood for "having taken the most part" in his defense.

Despite Joseph Smith's promise to free women of Eve's curse through the Restored Gospel of Jesus Christ and the women Saints' valiant support of him in time of need, the forces set in motion by politics and the press could not be stopped. Since the Church's beginnings, tales of unchristian behavior toward women had sparked political speeches and morality forums across America with the purpose of eradicating Mormon polygamy, a trend that continued until the turn of the century.

From such fulminating hatred, emigration could offer no escape. Journalists and politicians would continue to cast The Church of Jesus Christ as anti-Christian and to call its authorities enslavers of women. Novels and memoirs (given publishing of the day, often hard to distinguish) would paint Latter-day Saint women as exploited and shamed — the victims of lust and depravity — or as grossly immoral participants in a depraved lifestyle. Among four anti-Mormon novels that would influence another fifty-two in the nineteenth century, Metta Victoria Fuller Victor's *Mormon Wives* (1856) portrayed Mormon men and women as equally depraved and dreadful, managing to satisfy salacious appetites even as it demonized the innocent and advanced political agendas. In 1876, Ann Eliza Young, former wife of Brigham, would sell Dustin, Gilman & Co. of Hartford, Connecticut, *Wife No. Nineteen*, a highly sensationalized chronicle of her life with Brigham that drew the attention and profit she and her publisher desired. Reaching from across the Atlantic, the recently crafted character Sherlock Holmes took up the hue and cry in Arthur Conan

Doyle's *A Study in Scarlet*, presenting Latter-day Saints as intolerant criminals who forced young girls into polygamous marriages. Thirty years later, when he spoke at the Latter-day Saints Tabernacle in Salt Lake City, Conan Doyle would express regret over his misrepresentations of the Saints but stubbornly stopped short of apologizing.

Like the novelists and memoirists, religious leaders across the country would take the worst scenarios and write them large. So would women's organizations, including those devoted to suffrage and women's rights. As those battling polygamy joined forces with those warring against slavery, the Republican Party that fostered Abraham Lincoln would promise to stamp out these "twin relics of barbarism," building their 1856 platform accordingly. In an ironic twist, however, the National Woman Suffrage Association (engendered in the midst of the abolitionist movement in 1869) would, under the direction of Susan B. Anthony and Elizabeth Cady Stanton, join forces with Utah women who lived polygamy and support them in their cause for women's rights. In doing so, they would become at odds with the American Woman Suffrage Association, under Lucy Stone. Division would continue to carve an American chasm, where accepted constructs of rugged individualism combined with Christian ethos to sleep poorly with a pluralistic community and the Principle of Plural Marriage.

The political, socioeconomic, and religious storm that chased Joseph Smith and his church from Missouri in 1839 continued to brew in Illinois. Its eye hovered over Commerce, where Latter-day Saints objected to saloons and other gentile pursuits. Area businessmen pushed back when, in 1841, Joseph Smith became the first elected mayor and renamed the town Nauvoo. Illinois politicians grew genuinely concerned about the Saints' political reach. By 1844, when Smith declared his intention to run for the us presidency, with first counselor Sidney Rigdon as his vice president, state officials became intent on imprisoning him. Ironically, the local newspaper carrying the seeds of its own destruction would make that possible.

The *Nauvoo Expositor*, founded by a group of disaffected Saints and anti-Saints, had published its single edition on June 7, 1844. Bent on exposing Smith and other church leaders as well as controversial practices, the *Expositor* indicted Joseph Smith for practicing plural marriage and espousing exaltation to godhood. One of its proprietors, Francis Higbee, called Joseph Smith "the biggest villain that goes unhung." Offending Saints and non-Saints in this attack on the community, it concluded, "It is absurd for men to assert that all is well, while wicked and corrupt men are seeking our destruction, by a perversion of sacred things; for all is not well, while whordoms [*sic*] and all manner of abominations are practiced under the cloak of religion." The Nauvoo City Council wasted no time in deeming the newspaper a public nuisance that had to be removed immediately. As mayor, Joseph Smith gave the Nauvoo Legion orders to dismantle the press and, if met with resistance, to burn the building. As a member of the Legion, Grandfather William Moore Allred witnessed and may have participated in the destruction. He wrote in his journal, "I was present when the *Nauvoo Expositor* was destroyed."

This time, Joseph Smith could not escape. He was indicted for commanding the June 1844 destruction of the *Expositor* offices. His brother Hyrum had been implicated by association. After Joseph and Hyrum embarked on an escape westward, the famous Porter Rockwell brought news that a posse had gone to their homes to arrest them, bearing the governor's threat of establishing a garrison in Nauvoo until the brothers turned themselves in. When Joseph and Hyrum led a party of men to Carthage, Illinois, to answer the charges, the two men were jailed and charged with treason for having established martial law in Nauvoo; the argument that they had done so in order to stave off threat of mob attacks was never offered because

Justice of the Peace Robert F. Smith (who was also a captain in the Carthage Grays militia) signed a mittimus (a warrant) without allowing Joseph to contest it.

Some Church leaders opted to stay with their prophet, but his coterie of bodyguards was disarmed. Fearing for their safety, Joseph sent most of the brethren home, where they discovered that the Nauvoo Legion had likewise been disarmed by order of Illinois governor Thomas Ford. As one of Joseph's bodyguards, my paternal great-great-great-granduncle James Allred benefited from the Prophet's largesse. As Joseph entered his jail cell, he turned and gave James his sword, saying, "Take this, as you may need it to defend yourself." William later noted in his journal the implication of this gesture, that the Prophet knew he would not need the sword to defend himself.

In the Carthage jail, the Smith brothers were ostensibly under the protection of the Carthage Grays, a militia whose members had threatened Joseph's life — something Governor Ford may have known when he made the assignment. Willard Richards and John Taylor stayed with the Smith brothers in their cell. On June 27, 1844, John Taylor sang "A Poor, Wayfaring Man of Grief." His voice faltered with the weight of their situation and the aptness of the song, yet Hyrum asked Taylor to sing it again when a mob wearing blackface burst into the jail wielding rifles. Joseph and Hyrum Smith were murdered and John Taylor was seriously wounded. James Allred still carried the Prophet's sword when, immediately after the Prophet's death, he was called to load the bodies of Joseph and Hyrum, one into his wagon and the other into a wagon supplied by the Hamilton Hotel proprietor.

When the wagons carrying Joseph's and Hyrum's bodies rolled into Nauvoo, a crowd of three thousand (one of whom was Great-great-grandfather William Moore Allred) received them. Although he was only twenty-five years old, as a captain in the Mormon Militia since his teen years in Missouri and then in the Prophet's special guard, Great-great grandfather William fell into place behind the wagon, feeling that he had failed in his duty. He wrote about the experience in his journal, describing how the tears streamed down his cheeks and dripped through his beard so that the stock of his rifle grew slick in his hands. Members of the Nauvoo militia were desperate to find the mob and kill them one scoundrel at a time. But Willard Richards, who had been spared injury just as Joseph had predicted, cautioned the tribe of young avengers, "Think, brethren, and think again." The words kept young William and others from setting out to take revenge.

Meanwhile, James Allred had returned to Carthage and loaded the critically wounded John Taylor onto his sleigh. They traveled through fields and woods, avoiding the roads for speed and safety, arriving at Nauvoo in time to join the ten thousand mourners who filed through the Mansion House. The smell of putrefaction overwhelmed them as they came through the doors; the decomposing bodies had leaked so that people literally walked through martyrs' blood and fluids to view the mortal remains of the Prophet and Patriarch. With their deaths, the Latter-day Saint world had tipped on its axis. At least thirty-three women were widowed when Joseph Smith died, and several more became widows through the death of his brother, Hyrum.

Emma Smith literally could not bear the reality of her husband's death. According to Alex Beam's *American Crucifixion*, she fainted twice and left the room repeatedly before she could bring herself to approach the coffin. There she fell across the Prophet's body, crying, "Oh Joseph, Joseph, they have killed you at last!" Despite the stench, Joseph's plural wives joined her in mourning, as did the wives of Hyrum Smith.

But their union in grief did not hold for long. The centrifugal force that sustained their spheres of personal dignity and common connection was gone. Regardless of what Heaven might hold for them, on Earth, a single moment had changed everything. Many of the links that bound them as sister-wives broke. Some found those links re-solidified through marriage to other brethren in the Church. Others faded into the expanses of eternity. Emma Smith became an ardent spokeswoman against the practice of polygamy. Eliza, on the other hand, became the leading apologist of the Principle of Plural Marriage.

Death and tragedy had a sobering effect on all who knew Joseph Smith, but sorrow didn't stifle megalomania. Prominent people within the Latter-day Saint community, as well as some on the periphery, vied for authority over the grief-stricken congregation. One person after another declared his right to Joseph's mantle. The infamous John C. Bennett made his own bid for power, forming a fraternity called the Order of Illuminati, then joining forces with James Strang, who was in the process of founding the Strangite polygamous colony on Beaver Island in Michigan. William, Joseph Smith's only surviving brother, and the Smiths' mother, Lucy Mack Smith, joined with the Strangites, who later banished Bennett for sexual misconduct.

Before a large Nauvoo congregation on August 8, 1844, Sidney Rigdon claimed primacy as Joseph's first counselor and adjured the congregation to follow him as Joseph's reasonable successor. But Brigham Young argued that it was within the purview of the Twelve Apostles to name the Prophet's successor and called for a vote among them. Grandfather William wrote that Brigham Young "got up and spoke with such power that it convinced nearly all that were present that the Mantle of Joseph had fallen on him." Although Young would prevail, gathering votes from apostles serving missions across the United States and in Europe proved a protracted process and created a gap in leadership, allowing pretenders to the Church presidency to create upheaval and division among the Latter-day Saints.

Rigdon would eventually go to Pittsburgh, where he formed a group known as Rigdonites that first called themselves the Church of Christ and later the Church of Jesus Christ.

But the strongest contention for leadership of the Church emerged between Brigham Young and a woman. In addition to her stand against polygamy, Relief Society President Emma Smith, as the Prophet's only legal wife, insisted that her elder son, Joseph Smith III, was her husband's successor, and she presented evidence to prove it.

After Joseph's death, Emma Smith fell into grief and illness and often relegated her Relief Society responsibilities to other sisters. She was a pregnant widow who would give birth to her last child with Joseph on November 17, 1844. Because Joseph had been the trustee for the Church, Emma's financial affairs were tangled up in it, and with no clear successor, her situation was perilous. Yet her efforts to stamp out polygamy redoubled. She insisted that Joseph had renounced the practice of polygamy and that, excepting the spiritual ritual of celestial weddings recognized only in eternity, her husband had never engaged in it.

Meanwhile, Eliza R. Snow, generally acknowledged by Joseph Smith's elite circle of members as the Prophet's plural and connubial wife, also grieved deeply. She retired to her bed and stopped eating. She prayed that God would take her, too, for she did not want to live in a world without Joseph. After Eliza had undergone several days of solitude, her prayers yielded a visitation from her beloved to tell her that, while he had completed his mortal destiny, God had other plans for her. According to various accounts, she honored Joseph's direction that she must continue this "great Latter-day work." On the morning after this visitation, she rose from her bed resolved to carry on and help others bear their burdens. Her influence as an intellectual and as a woman soon became essential to the wounded church. Her poetry, when set to music, lifted sad hearts and bolstered faith; her leadership and spiritual gifts would be essential to preserving the heart of the Relief Society even during the twenty-three years it would be disbanded. In the years to come, she would set an example for Latter-day Saint women in myriad ways that revealed her confidence in the feminine divine: She delivered blessings liberally; she often spoke in tongues; her prophecies — whether truly prescient or a measure of the influence she quietly wielded — tended to be fulfilled. For example, Heber J. Grant was but a toddler playing on the floor of his mother's home when Eliza prophesied that he would one day be an apostle of Jesus Christ, a prophecy fulfilled when Grant served as the seventh president of the Church from 1918 to 1935.

My early life among fundamentalists who valued the exercise of spiritual gifts taught me to keep a close ear tuned to "the still, small voice." My father and mother taught me to pay attention to my dreams as potentially divine messages. I have considered the possibility that spiritual gifts involve the practiced ability to pay attention, to focus on and interpret telling details — what is today so commonly, even in medicine, called mindfulness. Through my communication training experience, I have come to suspect that all people have prescient moments or dreams. These proclivities may seem familial because they occur more frequently when the practice is imprinted early in life and regularly emphasized. Such inspiration and precognitions influenced Karen's exercise of agency in ways that would profoundly affect our family's trajectory, for they had influenced the development of The Church of Jesus Christ of Latter-day Saints.

As Emma Smith mounted her case against Brigham Young, Eliza R. Snow supported him as the successor of Joseph Smith and the new President of The Church of Jesus Christ of Latter-day Saints. Emma Smith had always treasured her children and promoted their cause, while the childless Eliza held fast to her hard-won commitment to plural marriage. Emma insisted that Joseph had blessed their son Joseph with the mantle of his presidency while incarcerated in the Liberty Jail. This matter of succession may explain why during the last eight months of Joseph's life, Emma had threatened to leave her husband if he didn't stop taking plural wives. The thought of polygamy may have become unbearable for this woman, married to a man her parents never trusted, whose only validation of her past and future depended on her belief in Joseph's monogamous devotion to her. Eliza, on the other hand, had not only reconciled herself to plural marriage but had become its defender, stating in one meeting: "[T]his sacred principle of plural marriage tends to virtue, purity, and holiness. Those who represent [Latter-day Saints women] as ignorant and degraded are aiming to bring evil upon us or they know not what they are doing."

As Emma Smith insisted on a religion untainted by polygamy, Brigham Young and his many supporters claimed another destiny for the Church, one that depended on plural marriage. Eliza R. Snow's strong example and her talent for negotiating, reasoning, and creating harmony were crucial to the emerging leadership. She had gathered around her some of the Church's most influential women, all of them plural wives: Zina D. H. Young, Patty Sessions, Elizabeth Whitney, Bathsheba Smith. They met regularly to pray, speak in tongues, and bless one another. They went out to bless and heal the sick and to uplift those whose faith and spirits were flagging. Brigham Young and his brethren defended the right conferred by Joseph for these women to claim such priestly powers.

But the brethren also needed to suppress Emma if they were to preserve the plural character of the Church. Soon after Joseph Smith's death, 43-year-old Brigham Young married

40-year-old Eliza—for time only, thus cementing her to the main body of the Church while she remained sealed for eternity to the Prophet Joseph Smith. The marriage of Eliza and Brigham is reminiscent of other political unions throughout history, two unlikely souls brought together to shore up power and public influence. Eliza's expression of metaphysical sensibilities through hymns and poetry strikes a stark contrast to Brigham Young's capacity for transforming religious ideals into material realities. But they respected one another; he became her adviser and counselor, and she enhanced his sensitivity. Apparently, their relationship, although cordial and dignified, remained cool and remote, for Brigham Young had more than his share of companions, and Eliza had already given her heart to Joseph Smith.

With the blessing of the presiding apostles, Brigham Young assumed control. To quell disorder and suppress Emma Smith's influence on the congregation, he immediately disbanded the Relief Society. As matters in Illinois deteriorated, Brigham mustered the Latter-day Saints and prepared them to leave Nauvoo. They needed to find the Promised Land where they could live the Restored Gospel of Jesus Christ without interference or persecution. Eliza R. Snow joined this cause wholeheartedly and planned to go west with the Saints in 1846.

When Brigham Young challenged the body of the Church to move west, Emma Smith chose to stay in Illinois with those who shared her disdain for polygamy. In 1852, after much upheaval and at least twelve different splinters from the main body of the church, James Briggs, Zenus Gurley, and their followers bolstered Emma's cause. A nucleus formed with two main shaping influences: resistance to polygamy and a belief that Joseph Smith had conferred succession as Prophet on his son, Joseph Smith III, as Emma maintained. In 1860, Emma's argument that Joseph Smith had wished his namesake son to

be his successor would be advanced when the new organization of the Latter-day Saints Church voted him as president.

Brigham Young's response to Emma had been to assume
the reins of authority within the Church and call her a devil for
her disobedience. The impact of the split reverberated throughout the membership. That the elect lady of Mormondom, the
wife of the Prophet and respected leader of the women's organization, would clash with male priesthood leaders seemed
portentous, casting a shadow that would follow the pioneers
when they crossed the frozen Missouri River in February 1846.

Brigham Young's dissolution of the Relief Society had
transpired with a simple announcement in March 1845: "When
I want Sisters or Wives . . . to get up Relief Society I will sum-
mon them to my aid but until that time let them stay at home."
His purported reasoning was articulated by Zina D. H. Young:
"He spoke of Union and said that it must be by this principle we are saved, by this the Saviour would come and reign,
by union the authority of the Priesthood stands, and holds its
Dominion." Considering the various forms of adversity that
besieged the Saints — from drought and plagues to mob violence and federal harassment — Brigham Young could no more
afford to relinquish tight control than could a ship's captain
on stormy seas. Internal discord could only sink the Church
ship faster. Yet the dissolution cast suspicion on all gatherings
and meetings among women, including their sewing circles
and visits to the sick and needy, and in effect stripped them of
their considerable religious authority. Previously, women had
conducted ordinations in the temple. They had prophesied and
conferred blessings. Suddenly such activities became suspect.
It is significant that women never regained the implicit priesthood authority (high priestess/presidential status) Joseph had
conferred on some prior to his death.

Some women were distressed about the loss of their organization. Even those who followed Brigham Young worried

about the proliferation of plural marriage. At least a few complained in their diaries — for example, midwife Patty Sessions,
whose young sister-wife, Rosilla, created a rift between Patty
and their husband, David: "I feel bad again he has been and
talked with Rosilla and she filed [filled] his ears full and when
he came to my bed I was quite chiled [chilled] he was gone so
long and I was so cold I had been crying he began to talk hard
to me before he got into bed and thretens [sic] me very hard
of leaving me Oh may the Lord open his eyes and show him
where he is deceived by lisening [sic] to her false tales."

Despite heartache, the sisterhood continued to do what
women have done for millennia: They nursed the sick and fed
the hungry; they bolstered spirits and shared grace. They loved
their men and their children and each other, ameliorating the
political and social forces that threatened to destroy the community of Saints.

Brigham Young had ordered his people to emigrate west,
beyond the reach of persecution. But they arrived on the banks
of the Missouri River too poorly provisioned to cross the Great
Plains and the Rocky Mountains. Church leaders created an
agreement with the Omaha tribe for the Saints to camp on
the west bank where they would build cabins and stage their
journey west. In this dreary settlement they called Winter
Quarters, located across the river from Council Bluffs, Iowa,
Great-great-grandfather William and his father, Isaac, erected
tents and built cabins against the cold. That winter of 1846–
1847, everyone in the camp suffered hunger, exposure, and illness, and 359 died.

Many of the men were gone. Besides those brethren lost to
the diseases of winter and of the river, more than five hundred
deployed with the Mormon Battalion to fight the us war with
Mexico. A growing number of men were serving missions

across the United States and in Europe. Often it fell to the women to stabilize the struggling community of Saints.

Despite Brigham Young's edict, the women persisted in meeting privately and in clusters. They saw what reorganizing could accomplish, but each time they gained ground, one event or another postponed reinstatement of the women's auxiliary. Yet they found ways to put their motto into action, meeting the needs of others and blessing one another as well.

Eliza gathered regularly with the women; they drew strength from and discovered great power in their sisterhood. The women shivered around campfires or in crude cabins under construction, and they prayed together for guidance. They put hands on heads and blessed and healed one another. They spoke in tongues and delivered interpretations. Eliza wrote of one visit to the Kimball home in her journal, "I spoke and she [Patty Sessions] interpreted. I then blessed the girls in song, singing to each in rotation." The woman tended to each other and to one another's ailing families. While recovering from a month-long bout of malaria, Eliza herself received care from the sisters she also blessed: Cornelia C. Lyman, Elizabeth Whitney, Vilate Kimball, Mary Ann Young, and others.

Together they visited the sick and the starving, the poor and the heartbroken. They lifted spirits and eased physical agonies and soothed emotional pain. Eliza made several journal entries during these Winter Quarters months: "In the morning met with sister Chase at Clarissa's — blest her little daughter which was born last Tu[esday]." Although the weather and the river combined to deliver sickness to almost every door, the sisterhood trudged on: "Met at Lyman Whitney's, stay'd in the eve., had a heavy shower of rain — went home with Loisa and Z[ina] in the mud rejoicing."

The women were sometimes prophetic in their blessings and prayers. In her diary, Patty Sessions recorded several experiences of spiritual gifts being demonstrated, including glossolalia (speaking in tongues) in the women's meetings: "Sylvia and I went to a meeting at Sister Leonard's. Only females were there . . . . I presided. It was got by E. R. Snow. They spoke in tongues. I interpreted and some prophecied [*sic*]." Patty Sessions was often in demand as a healer: "Tuesday, March 17, 1847: I visited sick. Mr. Sessions and I went and laid hands to the widow Holman's daughter. She was healed." Patty practiced healing by the laying on of hands when delivering babies or visiting the sick on her own, as well: "Sunday, May 9, 1847. In the evening, I was sent for and laid hands on Zina's child." Tuesday, May 18, 1847. "Visited sick in several places, anointing and laying hands on Sister Murray's son."

In her 1945 book, *In Retrospect*, Amy Brown Lyman, who became eighth president of the Relief Society, recalled a childhood event when she and her siblings were invited to pray for their mother: "Sisters [Eliza R.] Snow and [Zina D. H.] Young came to our home . . . to bless and comfort my semi-invalid mother . . . . [T]hey placed their hands upon her head and promised that through our united faith she would be spared to her family . . . . [T]he fulfillment of this promise was a testimony."

I believe that these women spoke in earnest, for I will never forget certain miracle events in my own childhood, particularly the Christmas Eve when our mothers roused us from our bed and brought us children to our father so that we could say goodbye; he had hemorrhaging ulcers and there seemed no remedy. We little ones sat on the floor and watched as the mothers formed a prayer circle. Simultaneously my father's brethren stood in a circle, each with a hand on my father's head and another on the shoulder of the brother before him. Together, women and men, they prayed for his recovery. I remember the sensation in that room, light descending and lifting me up, rocking me to sleep. Suddenly my mother was bending over me, smiling and crying at the same time. "He's going to live, darling! Daddy's going to live!" Does the power of body-spirit union really seem so strange today? Just look at how integrative medicine trends in ways large and small, incorporating yoga and mindfulness training and spirituality at medical centers such as those at Duke and the University of Maryland.

As the Latter-day Saints settled in the Salt Lake Valley, Eliza R. Snow and Patty Sessions continued to hold their uplifting meetings with small groups of women, but these intense spiritual outpourings seemed to abate after Eliza departed with the early group of pioneers, and the practice had nearly disappeared by the spring of 1848. Even so, throughout the Church's pioneering phase in Utah, women continued to contribute in unassuming ways. In 1851, a group of midwives met in the home of Brigham Young's mother-in-law, Phoebe Angell, to form the Female Council of Health; the women established a system of watchful caretaking through representatives in all but two of the city's nineteen wards.

In 1853, as the settlers' relationships with Native Americans were stressed by hunger, theft, and discord, Brigham Young reminded the Latter-day Saints that the Lamanites were the people at the heart of the *Book of Mormon* story and urged the Saints to offer them "the leaven of salvation." Thus encouraged, in February 1854, sisters in Salt Lake City organized to help Native Americans by providing them with clothing "to cover their nakedness." The pattern spread across the state and eventually included clothing the poor and new immigrants, as well. These local societies continued to function effectively until the Utah War and the Big Move of 1858. Eliza must have hoped that these "Indian Relief Societies" were a step toward restoring the formal organization of women, but she craved the intellectual and spiritual stimulation of the former Relief Society. In 1854, instead of joining the women who sewed clothing and put up food for the natives, Eliza helped her brother Lorenzo organize a Polysophical Society devoted to writing and oratory; open to both men and women, it met weekly so that members could present to and discuss ideas with one another.

An appetite for intellectual discussion was Eliza's birthright: Born in the aftermath of the First Great Awakening, which had celebrated individual rights and galvanized consciousness to spur the American Revolution, she was already inclined to explore great ideas. She had matured amid the Second Great Awakening, which encouraged spiritual life for all and gradually enfranchised women and other disadvantaged citizens. Her high-minded devotion to the Gospel nourished her belief in individual freedom, which made her one of the struggling church's greatest assets. Although she moved with some of the most powerful patriarchs in the organization, her respect for the validity of both men and women secured for her a quietly commanding authority, and in the Polysophical Society she was able to cultivate deeply reflective writing and oratory in herself and others. However, the harsh criticism of certain reformation-minded factions in Church leadership ("[I]t is a stink in my nostrils!" declared Jedediah Grant) led to the dissolution of the Society in 1856. But Eliza struggled on; despite health problems (she was rumored to have tuberculosis) she supervised women's ordinances in the Endowment House, a pattern she sustained for the rest of her life.

I want to believe that if Great-great-grandmother Karen had lived in Salt Lake City, she would have met Eliza R. Snow. Perhaps she would have been invited to various gatherings, broadened her mind, exercised her spiritual gifts, and deepened her understanding of life in the company of individualists like herself. Unfortunately, except for the occasion of her sealing in eternal marriage to Mads by President Brigham Young—who was often surrounded by female devotees—Karen probably never met the likes of Zina D. H. Young or Sarah Kimball, or any other woman in their influential circle of friends. In Weber Canyon, as it had been in Centerville, Karen's sisterhood was confined to quilting bees and religious meetings of pioneer women who lived on the threshold of wilderness. She may have designed a homemaking lesson or a Sunday school talk for her neighbors, but she didn't reach beyond Weber Canyon for validation or education.

Although rural settings like Richville seemed far away from the beehive of Salt Lake City, Church leaders maintained strong communication with outlying communities through Brigham Young's emissaries. John Taylor and Wilford Woodruff (both of whom would become presidents of the Church) made visits to South Weber, which places them in the Richville vicinity. Regardless of his stance on the Relief Society, President Young's plan for building Zion necessitated the help of women, and Eliza R. Snow and her sisters, as well as Karen Rasmussen and her sisters, did their best to carry out his orders in ways that honored the agency of women. Oddly enough, the disbanded state of the women's organization created considerable latitude for willing women to make individual contributions to the material and spiritual welfare of the sisterhood. The women designed their own religious lessons, their own social service projects, and their own homemaking regimens. In rural communities like Richville, they shared responsibility for the wellbeing of their neighbors, so they worked together and called on one another's gifts in much the same way the women of Winter Quarters had done.

In her rural community, Karen would have gone to church, where she and the other women still exercised their votes as members of the Church. She would have heard the bishop offer instruction from the brethren at Church headquarters, but without benefit of the Relief Society's reach, she wouldn't have known about the politically or socially consequential activities of Eliza and her sisters in Salt Lake City. Although it's conceivable that Eliza R. Snow and other upstanding women sent messages through their friends in Northern Utah to reassure and bolster the Richville sisterhood, the women of Weber Canyon would have been left to further their own growth, devise their own lesson plans, and teach their own classes.

The women would, of course, have heard Brigham Young's direction that the Saints organize cooperatives to provide goods for their Latter-day Saint brothers and sisters as well as for the gentiles who came in 1864 to build the railroad. Because the railroad was slated to run through Weber Canyon, the women prepared themselves to take advantage of the work made available as more than 5,000 Mormon workers and an uncounted number of gentiles descended to build bridges and trestles and lay track. Women in communities north and south took up the challenge and turned to marketing their needlework and produce. In the years to come, they would wash and mend the clothing of workers and sell butter, eggs, and fresh produce to railroad camp cooks.

With her many abilities as craftswoman and homemaker, as well as her strong Danish education, I think Karen had much to offer her local sisterhood. She might have demonstrated how to preserve fish with salt in the Scandinavian way — an acquired taste, but storable sustenance nonetheless, and a good source of protein and iodine for the hungry, especially railroad workers. She could have taught them to weave woolen rya carpets in the traditional Scandinavian style with long shag and three-strand knots, showing them how her ancestors had created rugs both warm and nearly waterproof, useful for the bottom of long-boats or for a hearth, beautiful as a bedspread or a wall hanging. She may have produced one of the earliest Danish carpets in Utah or displayed her creations at the Women's Centennial Territorial Fair. I do know her skill with weaving would keep her children fed in the days to come.

I think she would have given willingly what she could. But I have my doubts about her willingness to receive the aid of others. I suspect she was ashamed of her family's humble dugout and broken English; I have learned first-hand that unrealized shame has a lasting influence on one's sense of worth, springing up unbidden amid social events. She may have struggled with doubt that people would accept a woman who had been tossed out of her father's home. In any case, she bestowed on her progeny an inclination toward tackling gargantuan tasks singlehandedly rather than imposing on others. The tendency of my father's people to establish themselves with vigor and legendary impatience probably manifested in Karen urging Mads to build a new self-constructed dwelling in Richville, a home with four walls and rooms and windows to let in some light.

CHAPTER 4

Changes

WINTER DAYS in Weber Canyon were short, and darkness fell early in the Richville dugout carved into a hillside. Because of the cold desert air, catarrh plagued the Rasmussens, making them cough and snuffle their way through the day. When Peter got sick in the chilly cave, Karen hovered over him, remembering baby Laura's fatal sickness, fearing that scarlet fever or diphtheria or whooping cough lurked behind every sore throat. Their first winter in the frozen Weber Mountains reminded them of their homeland — different from the dry, open fields in Centerville — where everyone spoke a language of snow and ice. Yet the parched cold of Morgan County with its sagebrush hills rising to cedar and pine, its salt-laced sandstorms and dry blizzards, did not resemble the stark cliffs or flat, frigid plains of the Danish coast.

I can imagine how hemmed in Karen must have felt with only the meanest of creative challenges before her: how to keep little Peter from coughing so hard he'd throw up on his clean clothing; how to do yet another laundry in a tiny living area, then hang the wet clothes in the infrequent sun where they froze before they could dry; how to preserve their few supplies without inviting rats and mice to sleep in their beds; how to make bread from flour with more weevils than wheat. Food ran out quickly now; there was no well-stocked root cellar as there had been in Centerville. As much as Karen must have wanted Mads to hunt and fish, to do anything to stock the larder, she must have worried when he was gone. The terrible possibilities of wilderness — prowling Shoshone and Ute, hungry wolves and ornery bears, and the chance blizzard's sudden descent transforming sunshine to whiteout in an hour — these made her fret, and the children succumbed to her querulous spirit.

Early settler Thomas Jefferson Thurston had purchased some land for himself in Weber Canyon from the Ute tribe, who had long claimed the territory as their own. But bands of Bannock Shoshone now roved Weber Canyon, which adjoined their hunting and fishing grounds in the lush Cache Valley now overrun by white settlers. Neither tribe had fully deserted the territory by the time Karen and Mads settled there. Karen would have heard of the two Shoshone braves accosted by a farmer who threatened them with his rifle while they fished on his land. The braves had only knives, but the farmer died in the skirmish. One of the young Shoshone was imprisoned and sentenced to die, which stirred the ire of other starving natives. Karen would have wondered what the Shoshone might do if they came upon Mads alone, pursuing elk and deer on their hunting grounds. She had her own experience of the Sioux tribe that had accosted the Neslen wagon train company, taking their food and urging women to leave with them, and stories traveled through the canyon about bands raiding white settlements. Although she overcame her fear and befriended all who came to her door in need, she had to worry what might happen if any strangers — native, mountain man, or itinerant pioneer — realized she was alone, but for her children, in the dugout.

When Mads finally returned from hunting-and-fishing expeditions, did she meet him at the door with a blast of recrimination, as women in my family are wont to do when they love and imagine too much? Did Mads misread the smelting of her anger and passion, fearing that she aimed to fetter him with her tidying hands?

Both Mads and Karen took to heart the commandment to multiply and replenish Zion. They welcomed each promise of new life and were supported in this attitude by their neighbors. The small settlement of Richville had been established only a handful of years earlier by a dozen or so Latter-day Saint families sent by Brigham Young to reclaim Weber Canyon from the federal soldiers. Each family struggled with similar stages of want, but many of them already knew each other, and most of them spoke English. Karen could keep up, but Mads was proud of his Rasmussen heritage and was self-reliant to a fault; his struggle with English encumbered their social interaction. It seems that few of their countrymen had been assigned to settle in Weber Canyon. (Curiously, many Danish immigrants were sent to join the Allred community in Spring City, where they were plagued with attacks from Ute, Paiute, and Navajo.) Isolated in the Weber Mountains, Mads and Karen fought their way through too much sickness and hunger alone, unnecessarily sequestering themselves, given that the community of Saints stood by, ready to help. They each wrote long letters begging their parents to join the Church and emigrate.

It had taken Karen's father nearly a decade from the time he banished his eldest daughter from his house to resign himself to his family's devotion to The Church of Jesus Christ of Latter-day Saints. Karen's mother, Ane Magrette, had been baptized in 1857, before Karen sailed to America, and Karen's siblings joined the Church soon thereafter. Despite the many letters Karen wrote (according to family stories, although none seem to have survived) extolling the kindness and generosity of the Latter-day Saints, Soren would have nothing to do with the Church or its missionaries. Ane Magrette was both sensitive and intelligent; she did not try to impose the religion on her husband, believing that he would change his attitude if she exercised patience and respect. The strategy worked. Eventually Soren had enough of the harassment his children faced in Lutheran-led schools and of the town's boycotting the goods produced by the Sorensen/Petersen clan. Karen's description of the beauty and bounty of North America may have set Soren to dreaming about owning land where rocks did not impede his plow. Soren's eldest son, Baltzar, talked continually of his plan to join Karen. Soren made up his mind: He wanted his family unified and safe.

In spring 1863, Karen received the letter from her parents announcing that soon they would be leaving Copenhagen for Zion. Her lonely heart must have overflowed with joy at this news.

Whatever misgiving Mads might have felt about the prospect of so many in-laws descending on them was eclipsed by Karen's anticipation. However, joy was alloyed with angst as setbacks protracted her family's journey. The crossing of 657 emigrants aboard the *B.S. Kimball* from Copenhagen to New York would take a month and a half, two weeks longer than Karen's and Mads's journey aboard the *Tapscott*. The provisions aboard the *Kimball* weren't the best. At sea, sickness set in; the passengers and crew discovered that much of the food was spoiled and the water tainted. To make matters worse, the ship was becalmed for a time, and they ran entirely out of food and water before reaching land.

The sickly and weak were the first casualties. Ane Magrette and her youngest daughter, fifteen-year-old Ane Marie, sewed funeral clothes for several people who were buried at sea. After arriving in New York on June 13, 1863, the ravaged immigrants sat aboard ship in the harbor, awaiting the unpleasant processes of inspection and fumigation. This company struck a dramatic contrast to the jubilant, healthy crowd with which Karen and Mads arrived.

Once admitted to the United States, Soren, Ane Magrette, their daughters Mette Kirstine and Ane Marie, and their sons Peder and Baltzar (who brought his own young family), began their journey from New York to Florence, Nebraska, by passenger train according to Apostle George Q. Cannon's plan, but as they entered Pennsylvania, they were stopped and turned back because of Civil War skirmishes. (The battle of Gettysburg would be fought two weeks later, on July 1 through 3 of that year.) The immigrants were diverted through Albany and traveled along the Canadian border in freight cars, the riders tightly packed and standing hour upon long hour, their legs swelling and tingling painfully. They joined a wagon train at Winter Quarters, but the wagons were so crowded with the elderly and ailing that everyone able to walk crossed the Great Plains and the Rocky Mountains on foot. As they encountered the Uinta Mountains in Utah, Karen's brother Baltzar sent word via an outrider headed into Weber Canyon that their father's health had severely deteriorated. Mads traveled east along Weber Canyon to meet the wagon train at Parley's Summit and guided the Pedersens past the formidable rock formation called Devil's Slide and across the many small tributaries feeding the Weber River to arrive at last in Richville on October 6, 1863. Given that they had traveled approximately 7,000 miles from Copenhagen to Karen's home in Weber Canyon, the seventeen miles they saved may seem negligible; but for some immigrants, a few miles or a few hours made the difference between life and death.

For a time, the dugout housed a double handful of relatives. Remembering how I squirmed about inviting my own parents into my humble beginnings of a home, I'm sure Karen was uncomfortable about welcoming her parents into her hollowed-out hillside. Although only her parents would stay for some years to come, the dugout would still be crowded when Karen gave birth nine months later to Mary Catrena, who would be my great-grandmother.

Family members record that Karen had written many letters longing for her mother's kindly presence. How much it must have meant to Karen to have her mother beside her for this birth, if for no other reason than having her help in combatting the hazards of living in a dugout. Spiders nested in cradles; centipedes crept into sleeping mouths. The Rasmussens' neighbors had been eating dinner when a rattlesnake dropped from the thatched ceiling onto their table. Karen had been vigilant in the habits that would shape those of her daughter and granddaughter and great-granddaughter, daily sweeping webs from the walls and the ceiling and scouring surfaces until they gleamed. Karen had scrubbed everything she could and covered everything else with the rugs and weavings she'd made. How I wish I had a swatch of rya made by Karen's hand! I have friends who keep their grandmothers' handiwork under glass or in shadow boxes, but in my family, always on the run, little has survived our moves, one after another, often in the dead of night.

My father is gone, and so is my mother. I wish I had asked them some pertinent questions about my grandmothers. These days I fill the emptiness by paging through books illustrated with bright Danish heirlooms that stir a sense of heritage and longing in me: That bright red fringe against sand-colored tufts could have been made by Karen. I know that she would stop and look at it and stand a little straighter, her hands on her hips, knowing she was capable. She could keep out the damp and the cold by weaving such warmth. Still, she kept the door closed and the fire lit, for she could not bear to lose another baby to the desiccating winds that swirled from the Great Salt Lake into Weber Canyon. Ane Magrette's presence would mean an immeasurable safeguard against death and despair. And against something even more difficult to countenance.

Could it have been during that dark period in Centerville, after Mads and Karen had weathered two miscarriages and the death of baby Laura, that the plural-marriage Principle first loomed over their marriage? Their strong Lutheran backgrounds had surely argued against polygamy, making the thought repellent even while promising marriage and motherhood to Scandinavian spinsters. But soon after Laura's death, perhaps a bishop or stake president broached the subject of plural marriage for the Rasmussen household. The Principle was often instituted that way; after a few years of childlessness, a woman was expected to fulfill the Law of Sarah and find a Hagar for her husband. Had the brethren approached Mads? And did Mads approach Karen with the notion? If so, nothing came of it then. But if, Heaven forbid, they were to lose a fourth child, even though they had Peter, the prospect might resurface. And this time, Karen might need her mother, if not all her extended family, to argue Mads out of it.

Despite Brigham Young's support of women's suffrage, the men of Zion were not inclined to yield to women's sensibilities any more than they were to take a stance in the contention surrounding slavery. Most LDS patriarchs quashed female dissent, insisting that women were born to serve men, an attitude expressed by Heber C. Kimball soon after Joseph Smith's death: "The man was created and God gave him dominion over the whole earth. But he saw that he could never multiply, and replenish the earth, without a woman . . . . He did not make the man for the woman; but the woman for the man, and it is just as unlawful for you to rise up and rebel against your husband as it would be for man to rebel against God."

Brigham Young was impatient with whiners of either sex, but he had been especially dismissive of women's complaints about plural marriage, particularly when, in 1852, the practice of polygamy had been openly established. As patriarchal authority waxed to the point of eclipsing Latter-day Saint women's agency, some brethren in leadership roles began to rant publicly about any woman who objected to plural marriage for any reason. Jedediah M. Grant, who became Brigham Young's first counselor, preached: "[W]e have women here who . . . if they could break asunder the cable of the Church [the Principle of Plural Marriage] there is hardly a mother in Israel but would do it this day. And they talk to their husbands, to their daughters, and to their neighbors, and say they have not seen a week's happiness since they became acquainted with that law or since their husband took a second wife."

As in most cultures suppressive of women's agency, covert resistance and resentment sprouted and grew, emerging in women's diaries and journals and in their whispered conversations at quilting bees. For instance, Emily Dow Partridge Young wrote of wrenching inequities in her marriage to Brigham Young, "I feel quite ashamed to be known as a wife of the richest man in the territory, and yet we are so poor. I do not know why he is loth [*sic*] to provide for me. He provides sumptuously for some of his family." According to historian Jill Mulvay Derr, Jane Charters Robinson Hindley lived in the outlying settlement of American Fork, Utah, and felt a religious commitment to live the Principle, but when her husband "returned and brought two I cannot call them wives yet" could not help recording her anguish: "Oh what my feelings are this moment, life to me is not so joyous, it seems dark." Annie Clark Tanner, author of *A Mormon Mother*, describes the secrecy surrounding her plural marriage to her professor at Brigham Young Academy, Joseph Marion Tanner, in 1883 amid the federal anti-polygamy movement. Impoverished, secretive, and compelled to move repeatedly to avoid detection by federal agents, she described plural marriage as "an obscure and lonely life." But she also wrote of her plural life, "I felt the responsibility of my family, and I developed an independence that women in monogamy never know."

The year after their marriage, Tanner was called to serve a mission in the Middle East, founding the first branch of The Church of Jesus Christ in Palestine. He was among the first group of Latter-day Saints to enroll in Harvard, and he eventually was named the president of Utah Agricultural College in Logan, which became Utah State University. Despite his renown, the years of hiding from federal marshals took a huge toll on Annie, who was left to sustain herself and her ten children. Annie observes, "A woman in polygamy is compelled by her lone position to make a confidant of her children." Her children shared in her hardships and worked together to meet family needs. Her youngest son, Obert C. Tanner, shoveled coal and sold class rings to provide an education for himself, the latter enterprise blooming into a successful jewelry business; still, he could not bridge the gap he felt regarding his often-absent father.

Men and women who took exception to Brigham Young's policies had little recourse during the frontier era. T. B. H. Stenhouse, having served missions in Scotland and Switzerland, became editor of the pro-LDS *Salt Lake Telegraph*. But in 1870, Stenhouse and his wife Fanny were persuaded by the writings of William S. Godbe to criticize the policies and practices of Brigham Young, particularly concerning polygamy. In Zion, there was little room for disagreement with the Lion of the Lord, and the couple eventually left Utah to spend their remaining years in California. Each of them wrote several exposés of Mormonism, most famously Fanny's *Tell It All: The Story of a Life's Experience in Mormonism*, and T. B. H.'s *The Rocky Mountain Saints: A Full and Complete History of the Mormons*. As the Church struggled to create harmony and acceptance of the controversial Principle of Plural Marriage, the Stenhouses accused the female elite of Zion—Eliza R. Snow, Zina D.

Huntington Young, and Sarah Kimball, among others—of pressuring reluctant first wives into the practice. Disturbing as that might seem, Eliza and her peers saw compliance as no less an imperative for their mutual survival than obedience to a wagon master while crossing plains.

When the Saints arrived in the Salt Lake Valley, lost crops combined with the threat of federal reprisal and Indian raids to require absolute cooperation. Starvation, exposure, and attack threatened every day. Sensing the edge upon which their lives balanced during those first desperate years of settling the Salt Lake Valley, many Latter-day Saints bowed their heads and obeyed without question. But not all, and not always. Some women expressed their opinions openly; they wouldn't contain their criticism despite warnings from authority to accept plural marriage without complaint. Those who created contention among the sisterhood were marked for consequences, most of them subtle: lectures delivered by brethren who set their gaze on specific offenders, and the marginalizing of certain women by husbands and bishoprics and Relief Societies.

Women who were indiscreet or too outspoken were often ignored into silence and submission. Even to ask for too much attention might have consequences, as in the case of Emily Dow Partridge, the nineteenth plural wife of Joseph Smith who was later married for time to Brigham Young. Brigham Young fathered all seven of Emily's children, but because she was sealed to Joseph Smith, their children were regarded as Joseph's. In 1852, Emily's first child, Edward, died the month before his seventh birthday, an event that cast her into a deep well of depression. Brigham Young, burdened with many other families and the Church, had no time for her. In 1853, Emily wrote to Brigham, asking to be assigned to a man with fewer responsibilities. There is no record of the ensuing conversation persuading Emily to remain in the Young family, but she did so. She bore Brigham four more children. But in 1869, he sent Emily from Salt Lake City to Forest Dale, the dairy farm of forty cows that supplied cheese and butter for Brigham's enormous family at the Lion House. Emily's health suffered, and she was dreadfully unhappy there, as Brigham was with her, saying, "When I take another man's wife and children to support, I think the least they could do would be to try and help a little." Ultimately, life on the farm seems to have broken Emily's health, as Ann Eliza Young confirmed in 1874, saying, "Every one of the wives who had been compelled to live there had become confirmed invalids before they left the place, broken down by overwork."

Ann Eliza Webb Young was Brigham Young's nineteenth or twenty-seventh or, according to one researcher, fifty-second plural wife — depending on how one defines *wife*. She became the most extreme example of those women who opposed the polygamous hierarchy, and she refused to be ignored or marginalized. She sued Brigham Young for divorce in 1873, claiming neglect, cruelty, and desertion. She was excommunicated a year later and left Zion with a satchel full of stories about Latter-day Saint patriarchy and the practice of polygamy. Soon she was stumping through eastern cities with her book, *Wife No. Nineteen*, later revised and reissued with the inflammatory title of *Nineteenth Wife, Being a Complete Expose of Mormonism, and Revealing the Sorrows, Sacrifices and Sufferings of Women in Polygamy*. Although many of her complaints had substance and some of her stories bore truth, her words were dismissed as the vitriol of divorce by the main body of Latter-day Saints. Nonetheless, her account was quick to garner attention from the United States Congress. Her testimony has been credited with facilitating the passage of the Poland Act of 1874, which advanced federal prosecution of polygamists.

Militant exchanges between Brigham Young and the United States government had strained good will and intensified hardships for pioneering Saints, who sometimes murmured against their leader. During the Utah War, Brigham Young had made a revealing statement: "Do not be frightened because a few rotten, corrupt scoundrels in our midst cry out, 'O, the troops are coming, and that will be the end of Mormonism,' in order to deceive the weak-minded females." On the contrary, women had proved that they were not weak-minded, but industrious, intelligent, and remarkably influential. Through the years of severe abnegation, most women quietly continued to make a difference, just as they have always done. They ministered to the sick, met in work groups to quilt or preserve food, shared their knowledge and their talents, and honored one another as daughters of God. They could till fields and foster businesses on their own. Brigham Young himself acknowledged that if he wanted something done, he would call on the sisters to accomplish it. Despite — and because of — their initiative and capability, many of them voluntarily agreed to share their husbands with plural wives.

Most women who entered polygamy sincerely believed they were fulfilling the will of God. They engaged in elaborate justifications, agreeing that living the Principle was necessary for salvation and that plural marriage and the Church were one and the same. Such rationales did little to assuage jealous hearts or to extend family resources, but most plural wives claimed that they had chosen to live polygamy. In a sense they had; they could have resisted, chosen to leave their husbands or the Church.

Similarly, many polygamous men entered plural marriage from a sense of duty rather than desire. Several critics such as William Alexander Linn (*The Story of the Mormons*) and John Hanson Beadle (*Life in Utah*) have insisted that patriarchs' motives were lustful, misogynist, and megalomaniac, but many Latter-day Saint men who accepted the Principle as a religious mandate did so reluctantly. One obvious example is of Heber C. Kimball, the first Latter-day Saint man called by Joseph Smith to live plural marriage. In *The Life of Heber C. Kimball*, grandson Orson F. Whitney recounts how deeply Heber cared for his wife. First his faith was tested when Joseph Smith ordered Kimball to surrender his wife, Vilate, for plural marriage to the Prophet. After agonizing over this mandate, he took Vilate to Joseph, who told him that because of his willingness, the sacrifice would be unnecessary. Then he was ordered to take a plural wife. Again he agonized over the pain the Principle was bound to cause Vilate. At first, he tried to satisfy Joseph by offering to marry two elderly single women, but Joseph commanded him to marry Sarah Noon, a young mother of two who had emigrated from England on the same ship that brought Kimball home from his mission. Three times he was commanded before he obeyed, and then Joseph swore him to secrecy, warning him to keep knowledge of the marriage even from his beloved Vilate. The latter sensed Heber's agony and pleaded to know what troubled him, to no avail. According to her daughter Helen Mar Kimball, Vilate prayed for understanding, and in answer she was shown the Principle of Plural Marriage in a dream. She rose and went to her husband, reassuring him that he could enter the covenant with her consent, much to his profound relief.

My great-grandfather, Byron Harvey Allred Sr., wrote in his brief autobiography: "[P]revious to obeying the Patriarchal Order of Marriage, I was weighed down with grief on account of the trial it was to my wife Irene for me to obey that law. I felt as though I would gladly sacrifice my own life, if it would answer the end, than see her pass what she was passing through." In his autobiography, my grandfather Byron Harvey Allred Jr. also recorded his reluctance to live a principle "calling for so much heartache and sacrifice." He struggled mightily with the decision to take my grandmother Evelyn as his second wife: "[M]any times in my depression I would firmly resolve that I would put an end to it all—that I was not fit to live this great law." He wrote, "To undertake the living of that law solely for the purpose of sexual gratification, exacts a toll that no mortal man and woman will continue to pay . . . . It brings the added expense of support and proper housing . . . the immense cost of rearing and educating . . . children, and he has only just begun to pay the price. There follows the wreck of the first love." He also details the social scorn polygamous patriarchs endured: "To take more than one wife . . . is to incur the enmity, disrespect, and contempt of modern society." Public regard mattered greatly to my grandfather, who served the legislatures of both Wyoming and Idaho, eventually becoming Speaker of the House and Secretary of Agriculture in Idaho.

This is not to suggest that men didn't experience ego gratification, sexual satisfaction, and/or a will to power. And wise men recognized that a large and strong pioneer family could secure their success. For some men who worked hard building businesses and serving in Church callings to prove their economic and spiritual worth, being selected to live the Principle was a reward. During the last half of the nineteenth century — the years of settling Utah Territory and growing the Church — men with more than one wife could prosper in their religious communities and in the realm of civic influence. Of course, some men abused their families and their power. But once committed to plural marriage, earnest and devout members like my grandparents seeded their devotion with self-sacrifice and service, just as they did when encountering the hardships of forced emigration and mission assignments.

Mads would have been one of those would-be empire-builders who saw what was possible, perhaps reminiscent of his father's vast fields in Denmark, with tenants working the land, giving most of it to his father and keeping only a tenth for themselves. In the promised land of Zion, surely Mads expected to be a gentleman farmer and wanted enough progeny to work and occupy his lands. The Other Daughters Rasmussen confirm that he congratulated himself on the Danish noble blood running through his veins and believed himself destined for a superior life. On the other hand, Karen, daughter of a tenant farmer, knew to focus on practical accomplishments: a real house with windows and porches and her husband close at hand in the little town of Richville. But she would soon learn of Mads's grander schemes.

In that little village tucked into Weber Canyon, did Karen feel the sense of belonging she craved when she joined the Church? She had always been strong as an individual; what she longed for was to be herself in a community. Among those Danes liberated by the Danish Constitution, she had embraced education and the right to choose one's religion. She had defied her own father to follow her conscience. The glory she dreamed of as she crossed the Atlantic was celestial. But had her celestial bliss been manifested when she moved to a place sometimes cold as her homeland, but drought-ridden and strange? I'm certain that she participated in local activities and service — as would her daughters — and that when the Relief Society was again sanctioned, she joined. What reinforcement of her agency or support for her rights as a Utah woman did her sequestered community offer? I doubt she would have found a strong base for dissenting a commandment like plural marriage. What direction in anything but the most practical of matters would she have found for her appetite for learning? In the remote mountains of Northern Utah, she would not have even considered attending the University of Deseret in the Salt Lake Valley. Despite her strong initiative, she may not have realized that she could own land and be proprietor of her own business. These opportunities, which outstripped the choices afforded many women on the eastern seaboard where the national woman's movement had been brewing since the Revolutionary War, were peripheral to Karen. In the fertile soils of young democracy, the abolitionist and women's movements had sprouted and cross-pollinated, spreading through New England and along the east coast. Yet it would take the climate wrought by polygamy to bring a formal woman's rights movement to the forefront of Utahns' consciousness.

In the 1860s, activists and politicians fought to pass the Fourteenth Amendment to ensure that through voting rights, "No State shall make or enforce any law which shall abridge the privileges or immunities of citizens of the United States." The climate of the debate regarding franchise reignited the furor against polygamy. In 1854, *New York Times* writer William Ray had suggested (probably in jest) that female franchise could put a stop to polygamy, and many saw a valid logic therein. In 1867, the idea was revived and gathered steam; soon it was contained in a bill presented to the United States Congress. The initiative was welcomed by territorial representatives and by the Utah public. Dismayed by the Saints' inclination toward female suffrage, the sponsors of the bill tried to abandon it. But once *The New York Times* had opened the conversation about woman's rights and linked it to polygamy in Utah, the issue, like Pandora's box, could not readily be closed.

Surely this turnabout caught Brigham Young's attention. The economic and social upheavals catalyzed by the Big Move and the occupation by Johnston's Army had already emphasized the crucial importance of women to Zion's prosperity. Women had solved many family and community problems and had seized opportunities to exercise what agency they could. If they weren't tending their children or engaged in domestic tasks, they were bringing in the immense harvest of wheat, oats, and barley from the lush bottomlands along the river or working alongside their men as they dug the Mill Race Ditch, designed to divert water from the Weber River to turn a grist mill that took years to work properly. (The community struggle for a mill may have motivated Mads to invite his father, Rasmus, who had a mill in Denmark, to come fill the role with expertise. After visiting Morgan County, and observing that the mill wouldn't work because it was operating in dead water, Brigham Young finally intervened in 1866 and sent Ezra T. Clark to finish the mill properly.)

Brigham Young had watched the women of Zion as they civilized the frontier — with and without his direction. He was a powerful and practical man; as a fist opens into a palm, he held out opportunities to women that they had not enjoyed since the earliest days of the Church, as well as some they had scarcely dreamed of having.

Late in 1866, Brigham Young invited Eliza Roxcy Snow to sit down with him in his Salt Lake City headquarters. Although she had been married to Brigham the nearly twenty-two years since Joseph's death, their relationship remained somewhat formal. According to her journals, in the first moments of that meeting, she had little inkling of the enormous responsibility she would be asked to carry for the rest of her life. Given the prophetic sensibilities and poetic prowess for which she was honored among the Saints, and given the thought and prayer she had rendered before every decision — from joining the Church to marrying the already-married Joseph Smith — her spontaneous response was remarkable. At the time of this meeting, Eliza was sixty-two years old, a small woman with a slight frown of perpetual concentration, and still disposed to wearing the black of mourning. Brigham Young could not take Joseph's place in her heart, even though he had taken the Prophet's place at the helm of the Church.

In keeping with his direct and forceful character, Young would correct this respected icon of Latter-day Saint womanhood both directly and in print, just as he did any other person in his purview. In his candid history, *In Sacred Loneliness: The Plural Wives of Joseph Smith*, author Todd Compton explores the dynamic of Eliza's relationship with Brigham Young, describing how on one occasion Eliza confiscated the brightly-colored sash of Brigham's daughter, Phoebe, declaring it "too frivolous," but Brigham insisted that Eliza return it. As difficult as it might have been for such a dignified and deliberate woman to be upbraided before Brigham's other wives and his children, it must have been even more difficult to countenance his public censure. He would publicly criticize an article on resurrection she published in *Woman's Exponent*, asserting, "[It] has one fault and that fault is that it is not true." Six months later, Eliza submitted a retraction of her doctrine, expressing the hope that she had led no one astray. Despite the sting of public reprimand, Eliza's obedience to priesthood authority seems to have saved her relationship with Brigham Young from ill will. During family dinners at the Lion House, he often turned to Eliza, who sat in her place at his right hand for counsel, and sometimes he actually deferred to her.

When President Young announced that he had a new mission for her, Eliza declared, "I shall endeavor to fulfill it," even before she knew what mission she was accepting. Brigham didn't seem to doubt her capacity, although with her sharp features, sloping shoulders, and bright eyes she probably seemed more blackbird than beast of burden. Then Brigham explained Eliza's directive: "I want you to instruct the sisters." He authorized her to rekindle the women's organization, although he did not formalize her appointment. In fact, for thirteen years he refrained from ordaining Eliza R. Snow as president of the Relief Society. It took Brigham Young's death and the action of third Church of Jesus Christ President John Taylor to formalize the ordination of Eliza R. Snow as the second president of the Relief Society in 1880.

One might pause to wonder why, when the sisterhood was already engaged in good works through their own local organizations, Brigham Young would decide to invite women to organize at all, especially if he were still wary of women's collective power. Saints in general trusted their Prophet to be inspired by God in such callings. But being as pragmatic as he was inspired, Brigham Young must have connected the hammering of railroad ties in Weber Canyon to the mounting pressure brought by federal forces to subdue polygamous patriarchs. There was no question: He needed the women behind him.

When Eliza agreed to take on the challenge of reconvening the women's auxiliary, she embraced an appropriate outlet for her prodigious gifts and abilities. Her diminutive stature contrasted with the power and influence she wielded in the Church; she stood as the penultimate example of an elect daughter of God. Now, with Emma back east fostering a church led by her son and operating beyond the ken of most Latter-day Saints, Eliza stood as the first lady and leader of Latter-day Saint women.

In 1868, Brigham Young made way for Eliza's efforts to reconvene the women's auxiliary. He instructed the bishops, "Let them organize Female Relief Societies. We have many talented women among us." Over the next few years, he frequently expressed his appreciation for the capabilities of women: "There is an immense amount of . . . sound statesmanship within a community of ladies; and if they would only train their minds and exercise the rights and privileges that are legitimately theirs . . . they would find that they have an immense amount of influence in guiding, directing, and controlling human affairs."

This new attitude would empower the women of Utah to enjoy rights surprising to the journalists, politicians, and religious magnates looking to prove that plural marriage was oppressive to women. Even Karen Rasmussen, in remote Weber Canyon, might have been attuned to the movement. But having felt the slap of patriarchy — which stings, I know, as sharply in recollection as in the moment — Karen did not feel blessed in her assertive nature. Indeed, she may have expected that one day she would push too far and the bishop or her husband would banish her, just as her father had done many years ago.

Meanwhile, the women of Salt Lake City seized the chance to exercise agency and make their difference. Through that window of opportunity, Utah women would establish hospitals, academies, charitable organizations, programs for the arts, and social work systems, setting the foundations of a unique civilization in the Salt Lake Valley. Because of the railroad construction, Karen may have been more aware of events in Salt Lake City than were rural Latter-day Saint women in other far-flung places. Her hometown had access to the *Deseret News*, published in Salt Lake City. Otherwise, her knowledge would have been intermittent, through trips to Salt Lake City to attend General Conference in April and again in October or occasional missives from Relief Society leaders.

Karen's struggle for validation was probably at once harder and easier when she was pregnant. Because Peter was thriving, she may have sighed a breath of relief that any quiet inquisition into their fecundity would be silenced for a time, staving off any real or imagined pressure to live polygamy. Clearly, Karen liked having things done her way: no Danish spoken in the home, everything clean and orderly, a husband who heard her wisdom. But Mads, coming from privilege and at least as maverick as she, would have been just as committed to getting his way.

In 1868, had Karen been among the women of Salt Lake City who were busy reestablishing the Relief Society and thus engaged in education, business, and political activity, she might have channeled her willful nature, turning her energies to merchandising or artistic endeavors. She might have fostered big plans of her own if she had been exposed to examples like Sarah Kimball and the Fifteenth Ward Relief Society that purchased land and hired workers to build a Society Hall for women. In this simple building, the women could hold their Relief Society meetings in the upper story, which was also dedicated to arts and sciences, while the lower story housed commerce and trade. The enterprise was enormously successful, eventually developing into one of the world's first department stores: Zion's Cooperative Mercantile Institution, known as ZCMI.

The flood of opportunity had inspired Sarah Kimball to buy an additional plot of land for planting wheat to store "for times of need." Later the sisterhood sold their wheat storage to the Church for a tidy sum that the sisterhood committed to funding expanded programs and a larger building for their use. The Church and other entities came to rely heavily on the Relief Society's wheat program, which gave the sisterhood financial and physical resources to help during various crises such as the San Francisco earthquake of 1906, when the sisterhood sent sixteen boxcars of wheat and medical supplies, offering the first response outside of California to the disaster. Later, during World War I, the Church was able to sell much-needed wheat to the US government, all because of Sarah Kimball's foresight. The sisterhood used the proceeds of the program to fund community health clinics and educational enterprises. But by 1939, the brethren co-opted the program and the bishops decided how funds would be spent. This change reflects the general trend of the Church. Once it was established in the mainstream, women's financial and educational autonomy was absorbed into the patriarchal hierarchy. But it wasn't yet so in Karen's time. Pioneering and polygamy had invested Latter-day Saint women with a great deal of power.

Brigham Young challenged the women of Zion to educate themselves and their children. During the 1860s, he appointed women to head up normal schools (that is, schools to train teachers) that would become academies and eventually universities. The University of Deseret founded under Brigham Young's direction just two-and-a-half years after the Saints arrived in the Salt Lake Valley was coeducational from its inception, with as many women as men enrolled in college. Martha Jane Coray, who had acted as scribe for the Prophet Joseph Smith's mother, Lucy Mack Smith, was the first of many women to serve on a Board of Regents in Utah. The school she helped to cultivate, Brigham Young Academy, gave rise to Brigham Young University. Because federal land grants for educational extension services through the Morrill Act had not yet influenced the outlying areas of Utah, this initiative among the Saints was crucial to their communal growth. But in Weber Canyon, where the advancement of the railroad created the boomtown frenzy of all rushed enterprises, education didn't rank high on the list of priorities.

As de facto Relief Society president, Eliza R. Snow traveled to outlying communities in all corners of the territory — Ogden being the most feasible meeting-place in Karen's part of the world — and was welcomed by men and women alike. The sisters came out in force to hear her speak and welcomed her advice in choosing local Relief Society presidents. Eliza infused the women with her excitement and sense of purpose.

By June 1869, Brigham Young made his evolving point of view clear, declaring to the congregation and the world:

> We believe that women are useful not only to sweep houses, wash dishes, make beds and raise babies, but that they should stand behind the counter, study law or physic [medicine], or become good bookkeepers and be able to do the business in any counting house, and all this to enlarge the spheres of usefulness for the benefit of society at large. In following these things, they but answer the design of their creation.

Some historians believe that none of these advances for Latter-day Saint women would have been possible without the Principle of Plural Marriage. For one thing, women's suffrage and public health had become bedfellows, as women explored the importance of medical attention designed by and for women. American women had been attending medical colleges since 1849, when British physician Elizabeth Blackwell received her degree to practice medicine in the United States. But in 1873, after several complaints from women's leaders about deteriorating medical care for women, Brigham Young issued a call through Eliza R. Snow: "President Young is requiring the sisters to [recruit women] students of Medicine . . . . If they cannot meet their own expenses, we have a means of doing so." Brigham, who believed that women should attend women in female health matters, wanted well-educated Mormon female physicians to return and teach Latter-day Saint women to become nurses, midwives, and competent wives and mothers in the cities and in the hamlets and in the rural countryside.

Romania B. Pratt (later Penrose) was the first woman admitted to Bellevue College and the first Latter-day Saint woman to graduate with her MD, becoming Utah's first woman doctor in 1877. Ellis Reynolds Shipp, who began her studies in 1875, returned to Salt Lake City to establish the School of Nursing and Obstetrics in 1879. Between then and 1924, when it became Cottonwood Maternity Hospital (where my husband would eventually be born), the school trained 500 midwives and delivered 5,000 babies. Shipp bore her husband ten children and indicated that she had been able to fulfill her calling as a mother, a physician, and a teacher because she had left her children in the care of her three sister-wives whom she trusted to rear them as she would have done. Both of my paternal great-grandmothers partook of the nurse and midwife training offered through this Relief Society-based program and created careers for themselves while rearing their families, Great-grandmother Irene Allred in Bear Lake and Great-grandmother Mary Catrena Clark in Star Valley, Wyoming. Both were plural wives.

There's no telling how many women graduated from this six-month nursing program, but it extended well into

the twentieth century. Martha Hughes Cannon, the fifth
Latter-day Saint woman doctor, was the mother of three and
her husband's fifth plural wife; she spoke at the 1893 World's
Columbian Exposition in Chicago, founded the Utah Board of
Health, and in 1896 became the first female state senator in the
United States. Martha, known as Mattie, had closely observed
the effective planning and delegating initiated by Brigham
Young's call for female medical practitioners. As a state sena-
tor, she employed similar methods, assembling knowledge of
health care needs through systematic surveys and then insti-
tuting rules and regulations for a statewide Board of Health.
Her methods were so effective that the city of Los Angeles,
California, drew on her knowledge during the development of
its own public health system.

Some historians assert that Latter-day Saint women were
allowed to acquire the educational and civic freedoms not for
their own sakes but rather to serve the agenda of the Latter-day
Saints Brethren by altering the world's perceptions of plural
marriage and preserving the Saints' way of life. Regardless of
motive, in this regard the brotherhood stood up for the sisterhood. Apostle Joseph F. Smith declared at a Relief Society
conference, "By what process of reasoning can it be shown
that a woman standing at the head of a family with all the
responsibility to provide for them should be deprived of the
avenues and ways or means that a man in like circumstances
may enjoy to provide for them?" Some speculated that women
took advantage of an opportunity and leapt through a breach
in patriarchal strongholds to secure freedoms not only for
themselves but also for their daughters. As Presendia Kimball
said, "The day is approaching when woman shall be redeemed
from the curse placed on Eve."

My great-grandmother Mary Catrena Rasmussen was
only a toddler when Brigham Young called Eliza R. Snow
to educate the women of the Church. The remoteness of the

Rasmussens' mountain village made it necessary for the women to contribute whatever they could to public health and cultural enrichment. Karen would have had her children in tow if she traveled the thirty miles to Ogden to hear Eliza R. Snow speak about women's health, the suffrage issue, and the phoenix of the Relief Society. However she came to understand the issues, in her community she would have contributed what she could, sharing her experience of raising sheep and goats in rugged environments, of curing and carding fine wool, or teaching others to keep a hygienic house amid the dust and cold of Weber Canyon.

Karen's high standards and the close quarters of living with her parents made Mads eager to move his family into a larger house. He started the project alone, although his brethren in the ward had surely offered their help. How he must have dreamed of working alongside other Danes, for Karen would not allow him to speak Danish in front of the children. Mads's lonely progress was slow, and he longed for his own family. He must have heaved one of his great sighs before writing to his parents, urging his father to bring everyone to this vast new country, where immeasurable amounts of land could be claimed and developed however a man saw fit.

Mads must have painted for his parents an enticing picture of life in Zion, given that both his parents had ties to Danish royalty and must have longed to own tracts of land such as their forebears enjoyed. According to Annie, Amanda, and Alice Rasmussen, Mads's main motivation was probably his sincere belief that if his father would join the Church, the Word of Wisdom would lift his family's lifelong curse of his father's drinking. Mads never touched the stuff himself, due to his mother's cautions to avoid that which ruined his father's character. To attract his father to Zion, Mads postulated that Rasmus Sorensen Basse, known in Denmark as Soren Miller because he owned a mill, could establish a gristmill in the area.

Mads did not know that the Hinman brothers had recently joined plans with George Taggart to build a mill, and by the time Mads's parents arrived in late summer 1863, Rasmus was excluded from the milling business. When his own family arrived in 1864, Mads enlisted the help of his father and brother to build a larger freestanding house. He also had help from his brothers-in-law and whatever energy his ailing father-in-law could bring to the project.

Within months of Mads's family's arrival, the two-story cabin was ready for habitation, but it was a crowded house, with Mads's folks and Karen's folks and their own growing family under one roof. Rasmus still had trouble with liquor — to Mads's embarrassment, his mother's heartbreak, and Karen's dismay. After Mads's mother, Mette, died in 1865, Rasmus and his son, Soren, moved to Montana to run cattle; it seems they never did choose to join the Church. (In 1925, relatives performed baptisms for the dead, sealing Mads's father and mother and baptizing his brother, should they be inclined to accept the doctrines of the Restored Gospel of Jesus Christ in the afterlife.)

Although he was disappointed in his dream of a family business, Mads found work cutting railroad ties from Hardscrabble Canyon. Richville had become a supply center, feeding ties to the insatiable railroad. Warped or leftover ties were so plentiful that Mads used them to construct his new house, in effect his own cultural monument to the great race of the Union Pacific and Central Pacific Railroads to join the First Transcontinental Railroad at Promontory Summit in Northern Utah, linking the nation from coast to coast. The empire builder in Mads must have been awaiting that joining as eagerly as anyone. Plans were already underway to create special railroad ties of polished laurel and spikes of silver and gold to seal the union, slated for May 1869.

Brigham Young had reconvened the School of the Prophets so that they could advise him on economic matters;

he had engaged the youth of Zion in what was called retrench-
ment, so that their moral strength could withstand the gentile
influence. Now, by championing the Relief Society, he could
encourage women in home industry and the development of
cooperatives that would flourish with the railroad. The towns
along the railroad buzzed with anticipation, for railroad construction brought an influx of goods and money into Utah.
Just as Mads and his newly immigrated family had all the work
they wanted, Saints along the Wasatch front would build history and prosper from the commerce introduced by the great
iron horse. However, the anticipation of riches didn't work out.
Although Brigham Young had signed a contract with railroad
magnates, the Saints saw very little cash. The Church received
$750,000 of railroad equipment as payment on a million-dollar
debt with which Brigham Young planned to build a branch
line to Salt Lake City. Individual workers saw very little compensation. But the railroad brought a new feeling of prosperity
to Northern Utah. Access to eastern cities was more efficient;
social and political ideas began to intermingle, despite Brigham
Young's efforts to minimize the influence of outsiders.

In 1865, when the house in Richville was completed, Karen
surrounded it with vegetable and flower gardens. Sometimes
when she tended them, she would leave the children in her sickly
mother's care. More often, she would tie Mary Catrena to her
chest and keep little Peter at her side as they crawled among the
plants, searching for weeds and bugs and, later, harvesting the
vegetables. Karen and Mads planted orchards with scions from
neighbors' trees — the best apples and cherries grew northeast
of the Great Salt Lake. They transplanted raspberry and black-
berry bushes culled from thickets in lush Cache Valley; their
berries were especially delicious, for the cool mountain air and
sandy soil lent a crisp sweet tang to the fruit.

Karen couldn't have asked for more. But Mads's ambi-
tion — as his eventual holdings would attest — knew no bounds,

something the brethren would have noted. Was there an ongoing battle of wills? Did moments squandered in bitter disagreement make it harder and harder for them to salvage memories of shipboard romance and shared adventure? As he prospected for water so that he could make the sagebrush-pocked hills of Weber Canyon yield wheat or corn, Mads yearned for broad fields that ran to the horizon like an inland sea. Karen, with her own family surrounding her, succumbed to impatience with Mads's extravagant dreams, for even then he was talking about acquiring other properties — farmland up north, over the Idaho border, or a house in the budding community of Farmington where friends from their Centerville Ward had settled. For a time he may have counted on the prosperity promised by the Intercontinental Railroad that might push his holdings all the way to the great Pacific. Is that what he dreamed of as he tilled near the dead sea called the Great Salt Lake? Had he come to Karen with a handful of soil containing little bits of shell, gesturing at the lake, his eyes shining? "They told me this: It was once a great inland ocean, with fish the size of anything you'd find in our fjords back home!" Instead of entering his fantasy, Karen might have been more likely to shake her head and rub the bridge of her nose, a habit exhibited by too many of her impatient progeny. I can almost hear her brusque reply: "We need to bring in the cows. And milk the goats."

Although the inhabitants of Richville may not have known it, the issues surrounding polygamy and the larger world were slowly coming to a boil, bringing great economic pressure on the leadership of the Church. As Brigham Young cast about for solutions, his attention again focused on the many capable and dynamic women surrounding him. He had seen what women could do when they united in a common cause, and he considered the possibilities of female franchise: Only Latter-day Saint women could be counted on to fully support their brethren; only Utah women could change the minds of

Americans toward polygamy. One may wonder how Brigham Young could be confident that Latter-day Saint women would support polygamy, given some of the harrowing realities of plural marriage. But the most influential women of Zion were obedient to Church leaders and bore fervent testimonies of the Holy Principle. In fact, Eliza R. Snow, Zina Huntington Smith Young, and Presendia Kimball were actively recruiting women into plural marriages. Unthinkable among powerful and educated women? Especially among women who would play such a significant role in suffrage? Apparently, they saw no contradiction, because they believed the Principle of Plural Marriage was inspired by God. In Latter-day Saint scripture, the 132nd section of the *Doctrine and Covenants* would have it that giving one's husband additional wives made the giver a peerless Sarah — a belief that persisted in the fundamentalist faction my father headed and that endures in underground polygamous communities today.

Brigham Young chose these women to marshal the sisterhood in support of their beleaguered brethren, and they took the challenge with all their hearts. "I am glad to see our daughters elevated with man," said Presendia Kimball, "and the time come when our votes will assist our leaders and redeem ourselves." Through the efforts of these Relief Society mavens and with the help of national female rights leaders Susan B. Anthony and Elizabeth Cady Stanton, Utah women drew up a petition for the right to vote, and the Utah Legislature voted for female enfranchisement. The bill was signed into law by Acting Governor of Utah S. A. Mann on February 12, 1870, making Utah Territory the second constituency, behind Wyoming, to grant women suffrage. On February 14, 1870, twenty-six Utah women comprised the first female group in America to exercise their right to vote in a general election.

By allowing that a woman's place is everywhere she can serve, Church leaders opened breathtaking vistas for their

sisters. I would love to believe that Karen took five-and-a half-
year-old Mary Catrena by the hand and traveled by rail to Salt
Lake City, to the Great Indignation Meeting on January 13,
1870, where Utah women first demanded the right to vote, or
that she was among the twenty-six women who cast those first
votes in February 1870, or that she was in the crowd when
Susan B. Anthony and Elizabeth Cady Stanton addressed the
women of Utah, reminding them of their innate rights, urging
them to keep their franchise. But Karen was probably weeding
the garden, tending babies, and watching over her ailing parents; voting in a general election was probably low on her list
of priorities.

Whether or not Karen ever exercised her vote, nothing can
diminish the considerable agency she exercised in her rural
outpost. Her progeny offer proof that in her own sphere, Karen
was influential in the ways that mattered to her and, significantly, would matter to them: Although Mary Catrena would
take a huge step beyond Karen's carpet weaving through the
Relief Society's medical education program, she would teach
her sons as well as her daughters to quilt and make bread, instill-
ing capability in everyone around her. Karen's egalitarian bent
showed up in Evelyn, whose industry and cleanliness would
manifest uncompromisingly in all her children. Coming to my
mother's kitchen after a long day doctoring patients, my father
never rested on his laurels. As if through an agency of blood
(or, as Carly Simon wrote, that "silent understanding passing
down"), he rolled up his sleeves to cook and wash dishes alongside my mother. Not an insignificant legacy in the quest for
equal standing. Relevantly, in *Voices in the Kitchen*, Meredith
Abarca writes about the kitchen as the unexamined power base
of Hispanic women otherwise disenfranchised. Karen's male
progeny had, I think, inherited an appreciation of that domain.

Karen's parents had scarcely settled into the Richville house when Mads announced his plan to move his growing family thirty-one miles to Farmington, Utah. Karen would have protested that they had just made a real home and that her parents had been settled in Richville little more than a year. But Mads insisted that this move was what the brethren and God wanted for him.

Family legend has it that Karen's immediate reaction was to dig a deep trench of resistance. Did she suspect that the move the brethren ordered was what Mads already wanted? She knew his ambitions: He wanted more land and to match or exceed the wealth his father had once enjoyed in Denmark. She had just discovered that she was expecting again—the sixth pregnancy in as many years—and the very thought of moving may have made her sick. Of course, everything would likely have made her nauseated, for among the women descended from Karen morning sickness is an all-day ordeal. Karen probably couldn't explain even to herself the intensity of her reaction, although it might have made her suspect that the child would be another boy. Her girls seemed to have gone easier on her body than had her boys, who took everything they wanted and then some.

Mads promised Karen that he'd find a house in Farmington before he moved her and the children. He took their son Peter with him, leaving Karen to tend the Richville homestead despite her debilitating nausea. Certainly, she was not the only married sister in Zion left to fend for herself. Many Latter-day Saint women had to get along without their men. Although the Mormon Battalion had long since returned from their service during the Mexican War (some returning home to Salt Lake City or Winter Quarters from their discharge point in Los Angeles, others diverting to the gold fields and bringing a king's ransom to Zion's coffers), most men with initiative and promise were quickly commandeered by the Church and sent off to serve a mission.

But the other possibility lurked: Every hale and devout man in the Church stood — whether with dread or anticipation — to be asked to take a plural wife. Since Church Historian Orson Hyde's public announcement of the religious practice in 1852, plural marriage had been out of the closet, open to the scrutiny and derision of the world. Once reserved only for the elite of the Church, the spiritual promise of plural marriage was now within reach of any ordinary priesthood holder — including Mads Peder Rasmussen — who could support a plural wife without neglecting his first family. Karen would have understood this as well as anyone. In the Church of that time, men who prospered were expected to sustain more than one family. Indeed, prosperity in Mormon circles depended on one's willingness to live the Principle.

Throughout the first draft of this book, I was predisposed to fit the Rasmussen couple into the plural view of family that shaped my consciousness. Given my father's strong commitment to the Principle of Plural Marriage and that he descended from four generations of Mormon polygamy, I believed that Karen — being the great-grandparent my father claimed proudly — had also subscribed to plural marriage. Knowing little of Mads, I theorized that his sailor's appetite for freedom made him at best monogamous and at worst a bachelor at heart. I imagined that he sometimes longed to cut family ties and run away to sea as he'd done as a young man. This, I assumed, was what Karen might have felt most threatened by, and why I strongly believed that she had urged him to magnify his priesthood callings and live the Principle of Plural Marriage; I had supposed that she believed that this would ground him more securely to home and commitment, as it would my father and his brothers.

Yet it nagged at me that I had never known about Annie, Amanda, and Alice: three daughters who clearly adored and were proud of their father. If Mads had been an inveterate scal-awag (which would explain why my father's family refused to speak of him) my assumptions would fit neatly. But how to explain the ODR? Just as they had dispelled my handcart illusion, they now compelled me to reconsider Karen's attitude toward plural marriage. Was it Mads who was more inclined to see prosperity as contingent upon accepting the Principle of Plural Marriage? Had Karen spent her days dreading that she might be asked to live it? The proposed move to Farmington would have confirmed her worst fears. If Mads could acquire another home and plot of land while she remained in Weber Canyon, couldn't he just as easily acquire an additional family?

In the society of plural families, men moved in a curious state of everlasting courtship. At a dance or at church, any unat-tached woman could be a prospective wife, whether young, middle-aged, or old. Would Mads have longed for something to alleviate the thorniness born of being married to so willful a woman? No doubt, too, he might have craved at least some respite from the persistent press of their immigrated families and whatever friction that may have sparked.

Even so, once they were reunited in Farmington, it seemed that the couple might be happy in that lovely, tree-shaded settlement inhabited by four hundred kindly people. But the move catalyzed new disagreements and caused old wounds to fester. In 1866, after a strained pregnancy, George was born in the little adobe house Mads had found in the center of the village. (George is the younger brother who would become Mary Catrena's best friend for life; his biography would shed some light on the opaque lives of his parents.) The adobe in Farmington was much warmer than the log house in Richville; neighbors came to their door offering food and help and everyone seemed glad to have them in the community. Despite Farmington's ambiance, Karen would have been unhappy to leave her parents and siblings so soon after reuniting with them. Her parents would stay in the Richville house until their son, Peter, finished the little house he was building for them.

Mads may have been opposed to plural marriage in the past, but the events of 1868 through 1873 make it clear that he had changed his mind. Whatever their root cause, tensions between Mads and Karen must have grown with the twins that distended Karen's frame. She wasn't an inherently accommodating woman, and a belly so large that she could scarcely move about the house or tend the garden must have exacerbated her nervous temperament. According to family legend, the last straw fell when Mads, who was an inveterate practical joker, tossed a bucket of milk into Karen's face as she struggled to fit her belly and the butter churn through the kitchen door. She stumbled a little and struck out with the butter paddle before pulling herself together and gathering what dignity she could. According to the Daughters Rasmussen, she packed her things, settled the children in the wagon, and drove the team back to the Richville house. She waited for Mads to follow her. He waited for her to return to him, but not for long.

Could a mere practical joke have broken up their marriage? Would this alone have caused a woman pregnant with twins to leave her husband? There must have been a deeper, more intransigent fear at work. Even if Mads didn't speak openly of the Principle to Karen, she would have felt a pea of this size beneath a dozen mattresses. She would have known that their prosperity carried a weight of responsibility, the expectation that they should share their abundance with another woman. She would have had time to weigh the matter and decide to resist. Did Mads meet with Karen's stony disapproval by launching one of his practical jokes?

As I try to understand what would catalyze such a dramatic reaction to a nominal event, I consider surrounding circumstance. I know, for instance, that in Richville, the crops were under siege; a new plague of grasshoppers had descended, decimating the wheat and barley that had made Weber Canyon thrive. Had it not been for the railroad, the economy of the canyon would have faltered altogether. Certainly Karen worried for her relatives in Richville. But that can't explain everything.

Karen may have fled to the Richville house to shore up her claim to property in Morgan County where her family had gathered. How I wish I could turn to reliable records to help me sort out what likely happened that day so close to the twins' births! Instead, I have tales that differ from one family strand to another. From my father's silence on the issue, I had always assumed that Mads simply abandoned his wife, mother of his three children and extremely pregnant with his twins. Such egregious desertion was certainly enough to explain why my father simply didn't speak of him, a more potent indictment than blaming. Of course my father never would have suggested that Karen was unwilling to live plural marriage, for this would be admitting a female resistance to the Principle that simply wasn't countenanced in my father's family.

According to the ODR, Karen broke Mads's heart by returning to live in Weber Canyon without him. Mads then made a revealing decision: Instead of patching up his torn marriage, he took their eldest child, Peter, and departed for Idaho Territory, where polygamous patriarchs were wont to settle because they could elude the reach of U.S. Marshals roaming Utah. At that time, two of my Allred grandfathers, Byron Harvey Allred Sr. and his son of the same name, lived in that area, and they lived in a plural family.

In the Richville house, Karen struggled to make everything work as the twins' birth approached. Her sickly mother and father were little help; both had been ailing since their arduous journey to America. At this point, they had probably been installed in the little cabin their bachelor son, Peter, had built for them. Little Mary Catrena became her mother's mainstay; at the age of five, the child prepared linens and furnished clean water. I wonder whether Mary Catrena knew that her mother carried two babies, or for that matter whether Karen did. According to family legend, the midwife didn't arrive in time to deliver Karen's twins, a boy she would name Joseph Soren, after her father, and a girl she would name Ane Margaret, Americanizing the Danish a bit, after her mother. This formative and indelible experience may have set Mary Catrena on the path to becoming a midwife and nurse. (My own daughter, who became a nurse, was only three when my mother, who was tending her, was stricken with a kidney stone while I was teaching school. Instinctively, Denise became her grandmother's caregiver, wiping her mouth and emptying the basin after she vomited and soothing her forehead with a cool washcloth until I arrived late that afternoon.)

According to the timeline set in both the Clark and ODR family histories, Mads had begun the process of dissolving his marriage to Karen before the twins were born in 1869. When Karen did not come back to him, he petitioned for a civil divorce, which was a small matter in a highly religious territory. Church leaders approved his civil petition on the grounds that Karen had deserted her husband. But their temple marriage was another thing: As an eternal marriage, great sins must be committed, and prolonged petitions written, to dissolve such a union. Neither Mads nor Karen requested dissolution of their eternal marriage. According to the ODR, Mads wrote to inform Karen that she could have the Richville property whereas he would retain the Farmington property. He did not tell her that in 1870, in the lobby of a hotel in Montpelier, Idaho, he had met a Swedish immigrant who was selling farm goods; her name was Anna Gertrud Claesson. Mads told Anna he recognized her from a dream and that she was to be his wife. Anna and Mads were married in 1870, the year after the practical joke that sent his first wife packing. Mads moved Anna and his son, Peter, to the house in Farmington, where they quickly started a new family, the first and second children being my *raconteuses*, Annie in 1870 and Amanda in 1871.

I imagine that during the first year alone Karen would have yearned for a chastened Mads to come to her, pleading to see the twin babies she had given him; she hoped that when he arrived, he would beg her to take him back. In conversation, Aunt Rhea suggested mildly that Karen had been waiting for her husband to return, but she didn't elaborate and never wrote about it. (As a plural wife in her own right, Aunt Rhea's expectations from a husband had been severely reduced.) Sixty-five years later, my father's first wife, Katherine, would mimic Karen without realizing she did so. She and my father had been high school sweethearts and had married in the Salt Lake Temple. But in 1935, when Katherine had failed to dissuade my father from his intention to live polygamy, she stormed away from their Long Beach, California, home with their three children in tow, confident that my father would follow and insist on his family's return. Both women may have failed to understand the dynamics of plural marriage: Neither my grandfather nor my father pursued their first wives with apologies and pleas and promises. Instead, they turned their attention to building second and third families. My father filed for civil divorce after his first wife left him, confident that because their marriage had been sealed in the Salt Lake Temple, Katherine would be his wife in the eternities, if not on this earth. I wonder whether Mads took comfort in the same belief.

Now on her own, Karen had to make a living for her own children and help with her parents, too. Although Mads had given her a house, a team, and a wagon, he had left her no money and no means of support. She turned to doing other people's chores and making rya rugs to sell to the residents of Weber Canyon and to the patrons of the Relief Society Cooperative in Salt Lake City. I don't know whether she made the trip on her own, lugging her carpets, as she called them, along with her twins or whether she sent her wares with one of her brothers or a neighbor. I like to think she stole away for a day or two with Mary Catrena in tow, and that while she was there, she tasted the heady flavor of feminism, gathered with the sisterhood in the Tabernacle to hear Eliza R. Snow or Emmeline Wells speak. I like to imagine that one of her carpets was selected by the sisters in charge of preparing the Latter-day Saint exhibits for the Women's Centennial Territorial Fair to be held July 4, 1876. Certainly, Karen engaged in production and commerce enough so that she could have purchased a few things for her children and medicines for her sick parents — remarkable, really, for a woman of her circumstances.

After the dissolution of her marriage, it probably didn't take long for Karen to notice that many active Church members considered divorcees guilty of willfulness, shrewishness, and other character flaws. Had she been widowed she would have been treated with greater respect and offered help by Church elders. Widows were regarded sympathetically, and as a necessary burden; divorcees, in contrast, as difficult and self-indulgent. Karen must have longed for understanding, for vindication, yet her heart held out for Mads. Everyone, including the Relief Society leadership, was eager to see Karen marry again for the sake of order — and to eliminate any burden or threat she posed. I know the judgment she must have felt in their keen scrutiny, how self-doubt creeps into an alienated heart, urging regret. But not enough, apparently, for Karen to take the first steps to reconciliation. She stood fast where agency had taken her that day of the disastrous practical joke.

Over the next decade, Karen and Mads would each forge ahead and build separate lives; but wrenching emotional and physical demands would mar their peace. As Mads carried on with his new family, Karen allowed herself to be courted by a fine gentleman named John Cheney. Cheney came from august Latter-day Saint bloodlines, his father having converted future

Church president Wilford Woodruff and endured the persecutions in Illinois before going west with the Mormon Battalion to fight at the Mexican border. Ironically, Karen would enter Cheney's family as a plural wife. Cheney's proposal must have given Karen great pause; although John Cheney was very kind to her and to her children, and although she was assured that he would work hard to provide for them, I doubt she liked the idea of playing second fiddle to anyone, not to the sweet and welcoming Samantha Jane Dicksen Cheney nor to the shadowy Louise Maria Austen Cheney. But as Karen's days of loneliness, deprivation, and hard work continued, the prospect of marrying Cheney took on a luminosity she could no longer resist. In 1871, Karen accepted Cheney's proposal; the twins needed a father's presence, as did Mary Catrena and George.

Meanwhile, Mads's second family grew. Anna bore one child and then another, but she was lonely that winter in Farmington with no Swedish-speaking person near, so Mads moved his second family back to Montpelier, Idaho, to be near other Swedish converts. He acquired land in the area and commenced the businesses of raising cattle and delivering freight. His growing family required that he work harder, making journeys through the long, cold winters to deliver goods throughout the Cache Valley.

Beset with responsibility for four young children, Karen asked Mads to send Peter back to her, describing how much she needed his help. But Mads refused. According to the life story of my great-grandfather Arthur Benjamin Clark, corroborated by Annie, Amanda, and Alice Rasmussen, Mads wanted to keep nine-year-old Peter close for his new wife Anna's sake. Peter would keep her company and attend to farm chores while Mads carried freight, doing the family business. The Bear Lake area had long been the winter gathering place of the Shoshone. The Shoshone told stories about Chi-ho-bidge (a hairy giant who is man and not man) who wandered through Bear Lake wilderness; they told about the monstrous creature living in Bear Lake, a great fish or a water horse; those who claimed to have seen it could not agree which. The stories circulated among the Saints and unnerved Anna, who understood only a fraction of what she heard. She agreed that young Peter was man enough to ensure a sense of security during Mads's freighting excursions.

On an early spring day when the snowmelt tumbled down the passes, Mads set out for the nearby town of Ovid, which was surrounded by the Bear River and Ovid Creek. To reach the town, Mads was required to cross the swollen stream. Anna fretted about her husband and asked young Peter to follow his father to see him safely across the water, then return and report. Peter hurried into his boots and coat and mounted his pony. He spurred his horse and spotted his father fighting his way through the turbulent water. Peter urged his pony onward, wishing with all his heart to accompany his father and determined in any case to help his father as his stepmother had ordered. As Mads guided his horse onto the soggy bank, he looked back and saw his son venturing into the flood on his pony. He yelled at Peter to go back, but the boy couldn't or wouldn't hear him. Halfway across, the pony lost his footing and Peter was thrown into the muddy torrent. He surfaced and went under again. Mads waded after him, ducking and peering through the grit and foam. He ran up and down the banks, crying out for Peter. At last he took to his horse and rode toward the nearest farmhouse, shouting for help.

Grappling hooks to dredge the river were forged at Mads's own blacksmith's shop. Searchers dragged the river for nine days before they found the boy's body, which had been carried far downstream. They buried the bruised and waterlogged corpse in Ovid, not far from the deep, cold waters of Bear Lake.

Mads went to Karen and told her the bad news in person. Despite her strong spiritual conviction and her independent streak, she broke down before his eyes. According to George Henry's reminiscences as recorded in the Arthur B. Clark book and in his own life story, Mads tried to comfort Karen and confessed that he still loved her. But she was married by then, expecting her first child by Cheney, and she turned to her new husband for comfort. The next year, 1873, Karen's father, Soren, died and the family buried him in the Porterville Cemetery at Richville, and again John Cheney comforted Karen.

Word reached Karen that Mads was sponsoring a young emigrant from Sweden, Anna Maria Christina Ahlgren, to be a companion for Anna Gertrude, and that he had married her. Did it help Karen to know that Mads still loved her and that they would be together in eternity? Or did she, bearing two sister-wives with Cheney, wish that she had never left? As far as any record reveals, she didn't say. In any case, life went on, a series of small gains and big losses.

John Cheney seems to have gladly assumed responsibility for raising the twins as well as Mary Catrena and George. Although George would eventually live with his father, he reports that his stepfather "was good to us and anxious to see us get ahead." Cheney enrolled the children in school and made sure they had the clothing and other means to do their best there. Cheney tried to give Karen whatever she wanted, even to the point of riding miles to get her some rice because she craved it. Even though she was in her early forties, she gave him two children, a daughter named Achia (called "Axie") after John's mother, and a son named David. Then in March 1875, John Cheney died suddenly, leaving behind a prodigious family bereft of love and the means to live. At forty-three, Karen was a single mother again, a widow with six children to rear on her own.

After Cheney's death, Karen returned to her Richville farm. Even though her brothers offered whatever help they could, life for Karen and her children was hard. Her son, George, who was scarcely nine when John Cheney died, tried to make life easier for his mother by cutting and hauling her firewood and doing similar chores for the neighbors so that they would have a little money. Karen turned again to weaving carpets until her fingers bled. Mary Catrena learned to do all the baking and housekeeping and took on the care of her ailing grandmother. According to my father and Aunt Rhea, when Ane Magrette died Karen was so busy with her carpet-weaving business and preoccupied with grief she could not stop to make the twins clothing for the funeral, so Mary Catrena took charge. There's a photograph in the family album of a child in a white frock with a satin sash, beautiful and tiny as a doll's dress, made by twelve-year-old Mary Catrena for little Axie to wear to their grandmother's funeral.

When George turned ten, he joined his father in Montpelier; apparently this was an agreement between Karen and Mads, for she had given their son Peter to his father when he was near the same age. Mary Catrena was bereft; George had been her confidant and protector throughout the difficult years since their parents divorced, and Mary Catrena would soon be desperate for protection. Early in 1878, her mother was married again — this time to Peter Nielsen, a man who was not a member of the Church. Nielsen rented out Karen's farm and moved her into a sod house with a promise to build her a brand-new frame house.

No one living seems to know exactly why Mary Catrena told her daughter Mary Evelyn "things were not good" whenever she spoke of the time Nielsen was head of her mother's household. According to George's biography, "Nielsen did not like children, and he mistreated them." A friend who visited Karen wrote a letter, warning Mads that if he cared for his family, he should come and get them quickly. But Mads couldn't seem to get away, and the situation deteriorated.

Mary Catrena, who openly clashed with Nielsen, went on her own to seek advice from the bishop. Through the bishop's intervention, Mary Catrena relocated to the home of Arthur Benjamin and Helen Ross Clark, a newlywed couple expecting their first child. By September 1878, the Clarks had decided that Mary Catrena, who was pretty and extraordinarily capable, should become their second wife, even though she had turned fourteen just two months earlier.

Mary Catrena was already a bride when Mads made the trip to see his first family and found that Karen was still living in the sod house, with no new home under construction. He also discovered that Peter Nielsen had pillaged Karen's property, selling off cattle and small plots of land and mortgaging larger acreage, all for his own purposes. Mads helped Karen find a lawyer to set things straight. I take this as evidence that despite suffering from debilitating illness and preoccupied with his burgeoning young families, Mads still cared for Karen and their children. The new wife, Anna Maria, was bearing children simultaneously with Anna Gertrude, and his responsibilities had taken a giant leap as his health took a downward turn. Perhaps this explains why Mads was slow to respond to his first family's situation in Richville.

After she divorced Peter Nielsen, Karen went to Mads and told him she wanted their son George to return home, for she desperately needed his help. Again, Mads was tender and kind; he confessed that he loved her still, that he had never stopped loving her. Karen swallowed the great bolus of her pride and begged him to take her back. He nodded, and she thought they had agreed. According to Mads's daughters, the new wives agreed to the reunion. But when Mads went to Church authorities to ask permission to remarry Karen, the brethren refused. They said Karen had forfeited all rights in the marriage when she deserted Mads in Farmington.

In 1883, doctors advised Mads that if he spent another winter at Bear Lake, he would die. He must move to a drier, warmer climate if he wanted to live longer. On his way from

Farmington to establish a new home in sunny Arizona, he
traveled as far as Vernal, where health issues stopped him in
his tracks. That year's mild winter persuaded him to buy land
and make his home in Eastern Utah. He founded a freighting
company, relying on the railroad, the Pony Express, and the
Green River. But the next winter in Vernal was relentless, and
the work was hard. Instead of improving, his health plum-
meted. But he continued to work, freighting goods on the
railroad and the Green River, and he continued to expand
his family. In all, Mads fathered twenty-one children, most
of them surviving to adulthood. He took care of them as best
he could.

Had Karen embraced the Principle of Plural Marriage in
her first marriage, would things have worked out better? Karen
and her children would have had easier lives. Karen might
have been there to prevent young Peter's drowning, and Mary
Catrena wouldn't have been abused by a stepfather. Yet Karen's
other children and their progeny would never have been born.
Of course the tragic outcomes would have also been avoided
had Mads resisted the Principle as Karen had clearly wanted.
And perhaps he wouldn't have died so young.

As I weighed and fretted over what might have been, it
struck me that the strongest similarity between Karen and
me lay in our shared reaction to plural marriage. Surely her
leaving Mads wasn't simply about spilt milk. Hadn't she chosen monogamy as plainly as I, leaving Mads only when he
wouldn't or couldn't choose the same? Because of circumstances, she had been constrained in plural marriage — and set
in motion the family arc responsible for my existence. That
her third marriage — disastrous as it turned out — was outside
the Church is telling: She did not want to enter into polygamy
again. How I wished that, through some twist of relativity, we
could sit across the table from one another and compare notes!
She could provide the missing details; I could thank her for the

DNA and that inherited willfulness that has allowed me to lead the life she couldn't.

When Mads chose the opinions of Church brethren over "the love of his life," Karen added deep disappointment to her list of grievances: That the Church she had traded for father and homeland would reject her right to happiness with Mads and, more egregious, that Mads would honor the arbitrary wishes of local Church leaders over his love for her. She continued to attend religious meetings and Relief Society gatherings; there's no indication that she spoke against the Church. But thereafter, her meetings with Mads were brusque, all business. Karen didn't forgive Mads for putting religious leaders before their love until after his death in 1887; he was then only 51 years old.

IN REFLECTION

As I've become better acquainted with Great-great-grandmother Karen, I've realized that she has been with me always, echoing in my blood as I stood at crossroads, making choices that shaped my life. When I chose not to follow the path of my father and mother but to go into the unknown, I was terrified of losing the love and companionship of my family. Was it a blood-born sense of agency that gave me the strength to leave? Something deep in my genes must have shaped my conviction in the same way it had caused Karen to choose her new faith over her father and the protection of home. For years, I thought I was the anomaly, a sort of changeling, a monogamist in a family of devoted polygamists. Yet we had been driven by the same impulse, the same urgency: to choose a deepening sense of self and purpose over cowed allegiance.

I know that neither of us ever forfeited our commitment to family. When I chose to write about my secretive family, I hid at first behind fiction. But when my first thinly disguised autobiographical story was accepted, I was driven to tell my father about it, fully expecting his rebuke, even that he would demand

that I withdraw the story. I couldn't have been more surprised
when he gave me his blessing. "People need to know that we
really did live through these things — that they aren't made up,"
he said. Was that not Karen's DNA surfacing in him, urging
that we stand honestly before the world? My father made a
request: "Make sure your book is biographical in its nature." I
was stunned. As I tried to reconcile this sudden admonition to
tell the truth despite all the lies I had fabricated to protect our
family, another question overwhelmed me: How did he know
I was working on a book? I hadn't told anyone but my husband
about the pages I had typed and furtively tucked into a drawer,
which I always locked before slipping the key into my purse.

Eight months after that conversation, on May 10, 1977, my
father, Dr. Rulon Clark Allred, was murdered in his office by
the thirteenth wife of polygamist Ervil LeBaron, who wanted
to take over my father's following. This shattering event left
me holding an implicit promise to convert my novel to nonfiction. I struggled against a huge inclination to run from home-
bound heartbreak to Seattle or New York, to become a field
correspondent or a copywriter. But the pull of family kept me
in Zion. I was married to a Vietnam veteran and profoundly
disappointed by the sparse affections he was able to deliver in
our version of monogamy. I was tempted to end the relationship or at least to contain it.

Women of my generation were the first to have the Pill,
"the world inside a plastic box" that allowed us to make easy,
even thoughtless choices. But for some reason, thank God, I
didn't give up. I was surprised to discover that I could confront
immediate distress and long-term uncertainty without cav-
ing. Now I wonder how much of my commitment involved
a genetic predisposition toward muscling through. Karen's
most profound impact on her progeny isn't how she validated
agency but how she illuminated the endless complications and
consequences of exercising it. How can we ever know our

convictions are taking us down the right path? How can we ever measure the wisdom and cost of our choices while we are making them or even in retrospect? The best we can do is to have faith in our vision of what is possible, then squarely shoulder our burdens of risk.

Haunted by the losses of the Vietnam War, yet driven by the thrill of it, my young husband was restive and unpredictable. My veteran ancestors William and Reddick Allred would have called it soldier's heart; my Uncle Clarence, a World War II Marine, would have called it battle fatigue. Today it is known as post-traumatic stress disorder, a condition exacerbating the wanderlust my husband inherited from his father, a British immigrant. Now I see my husband's maverick nature in Great-great-grandfather Mads, whose yearnings could never leave him settled for long. What drew Karen and me so irresistibly to such men? Couples therapists postulate that people seek out partners who will help them reconcile contradictions of the past. Certainly my husband has given me the opportunity to do so: The ghosts of Vietnam and a postbellum thirst for crisis would drive him from the house at 3 a.m., which I learned was the time the enemy usually attacked. He'd take our only car and disappear into the night without a word of explanation. Sometimes he returned at dawn; sometimes he didn't return for days, leaving me to beg rides so I could get the children to daycare and myself to the junior high where I taught.

The 1970s were stressful times, days when I was afraid for myself, my husband, and my children. I feared for his life, that he might develop an addiction to drugs or alcohol or other women. I feared for my children's stability, emotionally, economically, and spiritually. As I began writing about my father and his assassination, I feared for our lives at the hands of those people who killed my father, especially when I found that I was on Ervil LeBaron's hit list. I struggled with the weight of providing for the family as my husband cast about for a career and a foothold that would keep him at home. I know the hardships of my life are moderate in comparison to Karen's, but I believe that, no less than she, I have always grown when I am most vulnerable.

For years, I suspected my husband of yearning to bolt. I worried about his wanting other women and recognized what an irony it would be if I ended up living what it had taken everything I had to leave. When I wasn't anxious about my husband's wanderlust, I fretted about his deep blue moods. I never knew, when I returned from a day of teaching hormone-crazed students, what I'd find when I entered the haunted house we rented (haunted, because I learned from a summons found behind the built-in buffet that children in the previous family had been abused by their father in the attic rooms, and rented, because for my husband, a mortgage was too lasting, too rooted, too heavy). If my husband's mood that morning had been particularly dark and deep, I worried that he had succumbed to survivor guilt and that I might return from work to find him dead in the huge claw-footed bathtub. At times I was so beaten down by his flashbacks and fierce temper that I packed up the children and planned to return to my parents' home. But I never did. Had some essence of Karen's hard-earned wisdom hummed within me, warning me about irreplaceable losses and bitter futures?

What caustic irony that the faith she risked all for would have the final say in whether she and Mads could reconcile! What resolution might have transpired if their reunion had been permitted? How differently might their lives have ended? I, too, have been at the mercy of the Church, but when my truth was told and my book was released, I wasn't cut off; the response was kind, even supportive. When my marriage was in trouble, I had a bishop who stood up for me and called forth something better in my husband.

Despite, or maybe because of all we've been through, I like to think that my husband and I became best friends and good companions after fifty-one years together. Might the same have been possible for Karen and Mads? Would they, looking on from that other place, be glad we stuck it out, relieved that we avoided what they couldn't?

⌘ ⌘ ⌘

More than ever I credit Karen's genes with urging me to bring my whole being to everything I do. Her conviction, along with that of other ancestors (particularly my maternal grandmother, Etta Josephine Hanson, who lived the adage that anything worth doing was worth doing well), brought seeds of individuality from the old world to the new. Here, in the Promised Land, the place members still call Zion, such individuality has played out in endlessly complex ways, in misery and in splendor. It has manifested in sweeping legends such as those of Joseph Smith and Brigham Young and in smaller stories like Karen's. These stories seem to turn on choices and contests of will, startling us in how easily things might have been otherwise. And always there seems to be an unseen force nudging us toward the path that stretches long into the future. Whether we choose to take it makes all the difference. Surely, as she faced her frontiers, stepping into the unknown again and again, Karen came to understand this.

Clearly, I inherited Karen's willfulness. Oh, my mother's Scottish ancestors were stubborn and intent, my mother occasionally revealing that streak of rebellion in her sweet personality. But Karen's openly headstrong nature thrums inside me like living bone made stronger through resistance. I am grateful that the polishing effects of life's tumult have effaced pride instead of love, and that gentler inclinations encourage me to consider that I could be wrong, or at least that I am not always right.

That, too, is Karen speaking, urging me to heed her own hard-won lessons — that the woman who must always have her way will be a lonely ruler, that love and respect matter more than control, and that we are ultimately accountable for more than we can realize in a given moment. The thought makes obedience attractive even to this rebellious soul of mine.

And I have inherited Karen's faithfulness, a bequest involving fidelity to oneself and others as well as the conviction required to step out into the unknown to discover something new and, hopefully, good and beautiful. I am grateful for the long bones that took those strides and bestowed a legacy of courage.

Karen lived to be seventy-six, exceeding life expectancy in that era. I imagine that her hands were worn and gnarled, probably arthritic, for this condition also has genetic markers. Partaking of a folk remedy that today has attracted the attention of the National Institutes of Health, she may have gone to her beehives and let herself be stung so that she would regain the dexterity to weave her carpets, tend her garden, and caress her children and grandchildren. Among these were her eldest daughter, Mary Catrena, and her eldest granddaughter, my grandmother Mary Evelyn, clearly made after Karen, both of whom lived large and adventurous lives and who deserve to have their stories told as well. They devoted themselves to healing and to tending the earth, and they taught their children to do the same. But this is Karen's story.

Despite her resentment toward those Church officials who forbade her remarriage to Mads, Karen didn't give up her faith in the Restored Gospel of Jesus Christ. But neither did she relinquish her willful nature, nor did she adopt the façade of being what Saints consider "nice." Since this book was written, recently posted family records suggest that late in life, Karen changed her name from "Rasmussen" and took an Americanized version of her father's surname: Petersen. In her soul, I think she retained a pioneer's commitment, always willing to brave the unknown yet determined to claim a permanent home in Zion. I suspect that she continued to speak her mind even when it nettled those she loved and to believe she was right most of the time. Her one acknowledged regret, that she should not have left Mads, became a legacy that many of her female descendants have embraced, holding firm to their first loves like a raft in a roiling river. In the mountains of Weber Canyon, she could not live wide, so she had to live tall, with the soaring faith that had cost her so dearly, shouldering accountability for every choice. I hope that she didn't fail to value herself and that her community valued her more than the record shows. Her gravestone, engraved Karen Cheney, stands in the Richville Cemetery, surrounded by the vistas and shadows she met each morning for the better part of her life. The engraving on granite declares that she died on July 10, 1908, which, according to weather records, would have been a day thick with dust and the whirring of bees, rich with the sweet sting of alfalfa and the awakening musk of sage. As surely as I have sought her, I believe that she lives on amid such rich and sensuous proofs of life, as she has in her descendants.

Acknowledgments

THIS PROJECT HAS required much time, mentoring, and caring. Those canny souls who sustained me in this process are precious beyond accounting. I'd like to acknowledge Judith Keeling, editor with a heart of gold, who caught the vision of this family story, cultivating it and sustaining me from beginning to end. Despite threats to her health and well-being, she persevered. You have been generous beyond any expectation, and I am forever grateful to you, Judith.

Thanks also to editor Renee Laegreid, professor, scholar, and artist, whose commitment to articulating the lives of western women has engendered this book and others in her series Women, Gender, and the West. Renee, thanks for standing up for me and championing my voice.

I'd like to thank Joanna Conrad, who has held the context for Texas Tech University Press through many iterations. Also thanks to Christie Perlmutter, who has brought her clear mind and natural precision to polishing this project. I'm thankful for Angie Miccinello, who clarified various intricacies in creating the index.

In acknowledging a historical narrative, one must not omit important figures from the past: I'd like to thank Karen for the adventurous spirit that sailed oceans and crossed plains and mountains and bestowed on her progeny this great and liberal life in America. I am likewise grateful to each of my immigrant grandparents and for those who came after Karen, carrying the seeds of light and life. I especially want to thank my parents, Rulon Clark Allred and Mabel Finlayson Allred, and my seven other mothers who had the gumption to live what they believed so that I could be.

I must thank my mentors: Diana Major Spencer, who taught me to stand firm and speak my mind; Sally Smith, who taught me that exercising honesty is key to sanity and enduring friendship, thus saving me from the lifelong pattern of dissembling to protect my father's polygamous family; Gail Della Piana, who introduced me to the gift economy of artistic communities.

Thanks to cousins, writer Lynette Allred Johnson and historian Sharlene Allred Leichty. Thanks also to my brothers, sisters, nieces, nephews, and cousins for sharing their diligent genealogical work.

I cannot adequately thank my writing mentor, Dr. David Kranes, who believed that my words should be put in print and required that I submit it to a wider audience in order to earn a passing grade. He has continued to support my writing while urging me to take action when integrity demands.

I am grateful for talented writer friends who read and gave feedback on this work, bestowing their intelligence and wisdom: Martha Bradley Evans, Lawrence Coates, Teresa Jordan, and Hal Cannon each proved to me that a writing life can be delightful and convivial.

I must acknowledge my longtime editor, the late Carol Houck Smith, who encouraged me most of my writing life in this project and others. Thanks also to my agent, the late Wendy Weil, who believed in my work. Thanks especially to my husband, the late Bruce C. Solomon, who made all the difference. In the loss of these three, I am now thoroughly orphaned.

Thank heaven, then, for my children and their spouses, and for my beautiful, bright grandchildren. It is especially for them that *Finding Karen: An Ancestral Mystery* has been written to reinforce this reality: Illuminating our roots allows us to find our future.

Love and gratitude to all.

Seeking Karen: A Bibliographic Journey

AS I'VE SOUGHT to be part of a family and to contribute to a community without giving up my sense of self, I've asked myself questions that may preoccupy others: What part does personal choice play in our lives? To what extent are we a product of our ancestors? Can we experience personal freedom and still be part of something larger than ourselves?

I began writing with the belief that equality—or the lack thereof—was at the heart of gender issues that struck schisms in women, particularly Latter-day Saint women, including me. As I launched into Karen's story, some magical-thinking part of me believed that I could dash off a book in five or six months because I had already studied Church and family histories in depth while researching *In My Father's House: A Memoir of Polygamy* and the second memoir, *Daughter of the Saints.* Plus, I had researched gender issues when I wrote *The Sisterhood: Inside the Lives of Mormon Women,* involving study that led me to realizations about women in the context of the Church and in the national struggle for women's rights. The discoveries I made filled me with pride in my predecessors. To prepare myself for the writing of this book, I re-read *Women of Covenant: The Story of Relief Society,* a history of the Latter-day Saint women's organization by Jill Mulvay Derr, Janath Russell Cannon, and Maureen Ursenbach Beecher. I referred to the Relief Society manual, *Daughters in My Kingdom: The History and Work of Relief Society.* I drank deeply of the preface and eleven essays offered by Lavina Fielding Anderson and Maureen Ursenbach Beecher in

Sisters in Spirit: Mormon Women in Historical and Cultural Perspective.
Martha Sonntag Bradley unveiled the Latter-day Saints' approach
to women's rights from the political activism of the late 1800s to the
anti-ERA movement of the 1970s and 1980s in her book *Pedestals &*
Podiums: Utah Women, Religious Authority & Equal Rights, ignit-
ing burning questions about equality and providing valuable well-
springs of insight and motivation.

Early in my writing career, friend and mentor Dr. Agnes Plenk
(who founded the first center for emotionally disturbed children in
Utah) gave me a copy of *The Chalice and the Blade* by Rianne Eisler;
Eisler's "partnership model" and "dominator model" formed a lens for
seeing afresh the relationships between men and women. Later, when
my husband shared a volume of essays edited by Paula S. Rothenberg,
Race, Class, and Gender in the United States, I realized how broad and
deep the rivers of inequality ran. When asked to review a Palgrave
Macmillan / Amnesty International book by British reporter Anna
Horsbrugh-Porter, *Created Equal: Voices on Women's Rights*, detail-
ing the plight of women throughout the world who are regarded as
second-class citizens or non-citizens, I realized again how much we
all have yet to learn and how blessed I am to live in the United States
of America during this time of growing gender-related freedom.

I also grasped the responsibility of people living in quasi-egal-
itarian cultures to enlighten and empower the entire human family.
That reckoning was reinforced by Nicholas D. Kristof and Sheryl
WuDunn in *Half the Sky: Turning Oppression into Opportunity for*
Women Worldwide. Viewing the world through gender-conscious
eyes put an illuminating yet disorienting lens on everything I
thought I knew. This new perspective opened new vistas, including
a look at the uses of power in Hispanic culture in *Voices in the Kitchen*
by Meredith Abarca. Gradually I realized that I needed to stop waiting for my own culture to change. If I wanted change for my sisters
in the Gospel, I needed to stop blaming others and heed the axiom:
"Be the change you wish to see in the world."

The leaders of The Church of Jesus Christ of Latter-day Saints
have clearly stated in *The Family: A Proclamation to the World* that
men and women are regarded as sons and daughters of God with
equally important but different roles. This statement and others in
the *Proclamation* have raised incipient questions: What does "equal
but different" mean? Is it reminiscent of "separate but equal," or is it

something else altogether? Is it possible for Latter-day Saint men and women to live in true partnership, or are they forever confined by the context of patriarchal hierarchy?

Gradually, I realized that literal equality is mythical: It is a beautiful ideal of playing and working together on an even field wrought in heaven, but it is something we are yet striving to make real on this earth. It dawned on me that responses to the context of patriarchal hierarchy, polygamy, and womanhood are a matter of agency rather than equality. Agency, the exercise of our birthright to choose, determines happiness or unhappiness. As a communication and transformational trainer, I've been keenly aware of the immense influence of choice on identity, whether by forebears or by an individual. The significance of making conscious rather than default choices can't be overestimated when considering how our decisions shape character and the quality of our lives. I have studied what happens when people chase after love and happiness while driven by resentment and frustration; such a pattern reinforces an unhappy paradigm through resistance. Those who choose to stand, accept, and work with what is real and present can effect transformation and joy. But transformation requires accountability, which carries the price tag of consciousness.

I had been a communication and human development facilitator for thirty-five years. Even though I have done my best to practice what I preach and lead an accountable life, I still felt peculiar in my family, an anomaly in the religious group of my youth, and marginalized in both the fundamentalist community and the mainstream Church. For the sake of accountability, I appreciate the Latter-day Saint tenet of foreordination, which indicates that we essentially choose the family into which we are born. Given a grand design, where tendencies are bestowed as well as chosen, I pondered why I would choose uncompromising individuality even though my rebellious streak alienated me from the warm fires of home and family. Why harbor a proclivity to stir up hidden things that offend those I love? Why, I asked myself, can't I just leave things alone? A yearning to know my place sent me searching libraries, genealogical websites, and family histories. I wrote about my discoveries to find out what I was thinking and feeling in the hope that I could be more conscientious in my choices. I hoped to find an ancestral woman who could teach me about her life and mine and thus reveal where I fit in the enormous family and the religion to which, it seemed, I owed my life. It was my "handcart grandmother" who called back to me, the pioneer in my father's line, the one, he said, who "suffered many things" and "endured to the end." The one he called Grandmother Karen.

Latter-day Saints are a devoutly record-keeping people. Even before the glut of the Information Age, we enjoyed an embarrassment of riches. Extensive archives through Latter-day Saint Church history and BYU Library websites (and some maintained in my family's library) include such resources as Joseph Smith's *History of the Church, Times and Seasons,* and *Journal of Discourses* Volumes 1–26, and a vast array of immigration and ancestral records, notably the Mormon Migration Database, which links to myriad records and journals. The Church's remarkable educational programs are available through the website, allowing access to eloquent and well-organized lesson manuals that provide history and doctrine as well as life lessons calibrated from different angles for different audiences while delivering substance in simple, comprehensible ways. Several newspapers and books have also been helpful, particularly the Utah-based papers *Deseret News* and *The Salt Lake Tribune.* Jan Shipps's *Mormonism: The Story of a New Religious Tradition* and Richard Lyman Bushman's *Mormonism: A Very Short Introduction* provided panoramas of the culture, especially important for someone like me who has been raised with a canted perspective of Latter-day Saint history. A valuable book written by historians Leonard J. Arrington and Davis Bitton, *The Mormon Experience: A History of the Latter-day Saints,* expands one's sense of history unfolding. I wish I had accessed Daniel H. Ludlow's five-volume *Encyclopedia of Mormonism* when I wrote my previous books; my writings would have been more accurate — easier to write and to read.

Turning to family histories, I rejoiced again that the men in my family are diligent journalists. Great-great-grandfather William Moore Allred, Great-grandfather Byron Harvey Allred Sr., Grandfather Arthur Benjamin Clark, Grandfather Byron Harvey Jr., and my father, Dr. Rulon Clark Allred, all left autobiographies and journals that rendered personal, Latter-day Saint, and American history in living color. I knew about the great-great-uncle, a member of the Mormon Battalion and a rescuer of the Willie and Martin Handcart Company, who recorded his experiences in *The Diary of Reddick N. Allred,* leaving vivid stories often retold by family members and Church leaders. But Reddick Allred knew little or nothing of Grandmother Karen, who immigrated to Utah a decade after his advent into the Great Salt Lake Valley and whose family did not join with his until 1874.

My initial acquaintance with the history of Karen and Mads Rasmussen came from my great-grandfather's book of remembrance, *The Life of Arthur Benjamin Clark and His Descendants*. The material produced by my father's half-sister, Rhea Allred Kunz, in *Voices of Women: Approbating Celestial or Plural Marriage*, provided rare female perspectives. I am thankful for Aunt Rhea's courage and generosity of spirit in submitting to interviews with me before her death and in writing about the family of her father's plural wife even though she had no direct blood-tie to my grandmothers Karen, Mary Catrena, and Evelyn.

But records of most of my female ancestors were not readily accessible. Girls and women of today's Church and even those of fundamentalist persuasion have been encouraged to keep journals and trace their ancestry. But it wasn't always the case. My grand-mothers and great-grandmothers didn't keep consistent diaries even though they were educated and articulate. My desire to write about women who don't or can't speak for themselves is an extension of my relationship with my reserved and deeply sensitive mother. Speaking up for her, asserting her rights and standing up for what she truly wanted, was good practice for writing this book. I've tried to build a nest for those silent voices through intuition and imagination, using whatever twigs and threads are available.

Still, the dearth of material written by female ancestors about their own lives — particularly Great-great-grandmother Karen Sorensen Rasmussen — gnawed at my heart as I researched and wrote. Why didn't those women see how valuable their record would be not only for their daughters and granddaughters but for all people? Did they devalue themselves? Were they too busy being "Marthas" instead of "Marys," or were they wrapped in secrecy, afraid their journals would be used against them? Although these women were literate, circum-stance alone compelled them to focus on meeting primary needs. As Virginia Woolf points out in *A Room of One's Own*, well-situated ladies then and now who have the leisure and space to call their own are more inclined to write their lives than those who must spend their days on housework and eking out a living.

Oral accounts from parents, siblings, and cousins have been valu-able in my discovering purpose and attitude, even when information

was less than accurate. My father spoke proudly of his great-grandmother Karen and her ordeal as she pulled a handcart across the
Great Plains. He didn't speak of his great-grandfather Mads, however; I suspect he harbored judgment and some defensive or evasive
attitudes about a man who would divorce his pregnant-with-twins
wife and leave her to raise five young children alone. (This notion is
especially interesting in light of my father's having driven his own
first wife to leave him with three children to raise on her own as he
pursued his destiny as a polygamous patriarch.) My grandmother,
my aunt, and my father's wives spoke about Karen and her daughter,
Mary Catrena. These women etched an impression of sharp intelligence and impatience, traits underscored in Grandmother Evelyn's
character and manifested in my father's tendency to bite his words
and rush from one thing to another. Grandmother Evelyn's personality is stamped on me like a brand. She owns one of the voices in my
head, the one that reminds me to stop blaming circumstances and
other people, that it's up to me and God.

My father's two-volume genealogy, *The Allred Family in
America*, yielded a first glimpse into the rich and varied lineage of
our ancestry, marked as it is with martyr's complex. My father traced
our line back to the Archbishop of York who crowned William the
Conqueror the king of the Britons and who, it is said, died of a
broken heart when William reneged on his promises and ravaged
church property, taking everything of value. I know that there are
flaws in my father's attempt to render a comprehensive genealogy,
but it has provided a strong foundation for subsequent research. The
official publication of the Allred Family Organization, the *Allred
Family Newsletter*, has done much to clarify family history, including general information, biographical sketches of family members,
and verification of family lines through DNA testing. I am grateful
to those who recorded, edited, and preserved these precious records
for their progeny.

Despite these supporting accounts of Karen's life, I have wished
and wished that she had written a diary! Without her voice, I was
required to rely on peripheral information — scholarly treatises, pioneer stories, and rare journals of other Latter-day Saints of the time,
including a few journals provided (mostly by men) of what it was
like to convert to The Church of Jesus Christ of Latter-day Saints
in predominantly Lutheran Scandinavia. The scandalized response

of most Nordic people to plural marriage underscores her father's legendary reaction to Karen's conversion, which I found in excerpts from the *Torkel E. Torkelson Autobiography* cited in *Polygamy among the Norwegian Saints*, by Helge Seljaas.

Through the Church History Library, the Mormon Overland Travel Database, and Brigham Young University's online library, I found a plethora of immigration records, including journals of passengers on a steamer carrying Scandinavian Saints across the stormy North Sea to Grimsby, England, with 355 Latter-day Saints aboard, most of them newly baptized Scandinavians, and a manifest and 1859 voyage records for the *William Tapscott*. An article published in *The New York Herald* on June 14, 1859, listed Mads Peter and Karen Sorensen Rasmussen among the passengers and mentioned the marriage of nineteen couples aboard ship. A more dismissive account in *The New York Times* sketchily corroborates the *Herald*'s account.

I found a rich history of packet ships through Basil Lubbock's *The Western Ocean Packets* and Conway B. Sonne's *Ships, Saints, and Mariners: A Maritime Encyclopedia of Mormon Migration, 1830–1890*. Kirsten Sorenson's online article, "Shipwrecked Saints Intrigue Curator: Display of artifacts planned, survivors' descendants sought" described the wreck of the *Julia Ann* against a coral reef near the Society Islands in 1855, killing five Saints, thus vivifying the danger of ocean travel while emphasizing the extraordinary Latter-day Saint track record of successful voyages.

President Robert Neslen, who organized the company, arranged for the immigrants' passage, and supervised their work groups, summed up the voyage in a fascinating letter to a Latter-day Saint leader, Asa Calkin, which was published in the Latter-day Saints' periodical *Millennial Star*, June 18, 1859. Neslen also organized the overland trek of his company, which he finalized with a report to Brigham Young and his colleagues.

I learned about the Perpetual Emigration Fund from various Latter-day Saint histories such as *The Story of the Latter-day Saints*, by James B. Allen and Glen M. Leonard, as well as from personal records and journals of Scandinavian and British converts. I was delighted to discover narratives from passengers on the 1859 voyage of the *William Tapscott*. For instance, the *Journal of Henry Hobbs, 1835–1917*, provided vivid descriptions of events such as boarding, sailing, and arriving in New York; struggles with weather; lists of supplies; and detailed and colorful quotidian entries that gave me a fully dimensioned impression of life aboard the packet ship.

I had heard stories of Great-great-grandmother Karen's privations; *The Life of Mons Larson*, compiled by his daughter Ellen Johanna Larson Smith, confirms that all five companies, whether handcart or wagon train, suffered during the trek. This short biography clarified events, including poor management of company supplies that led to desperate hunger and the miraculous stack of bread discovered beneath a tree, manna from heaven in America. *The Mourits Mouritsen Family: A Record of His Posterity and His Ancestors*, compiled and edited by Carrie Mouritsen Jones and Jerald Olean Seelos, a well-written account tracing the voyage from Copenhagen to New York and the journey to Salt Lake City, includes peripheral history that places Mouritsen's journey in context. Also helpful were the James Stephen Brown journal, the William Henry Jarvis Family Migration story, and Matthias Nielsen's recollections. All were available at the Mormon Migration Database through the Brigham Young University Library online.

For perspective, I looked beyond annals of the faithful into research published by the Danish Society for Emigration History in collaboration with Danes Worldwide Archives. A mentor from my University of Utah undergraduate days, William Mulder, provides a clear-eyed account of the Latter-day Saints in America through *The Mormons in American History* and *Homeward to Zion: The Mormon Migration from Scandinavia*. Also valuable is an older book preserving many details that otherwise would have been lost: Authored primarily by Andrew Jenson, *History of the Scandinavian Mission* provides insight into the struggles of missionaries, converts, and the challenge of translating the scriptures. Edith Matteson and Jean Matteson co-authored *Mormon Influence on Scandinavian Settlement in Nebraska*, which shows the impact of Winter Quarters on immigrants who were stalled by bad weather or penury.

The Mattesons also provided insight into the general disgruntlement that caused some Scandinavian Saints to abandon their westward trek. Tempers erupted when Scandinavians who wanted to settle in Nebraska reneged on the "pay it forward" provision of their Perpetual Emigration grants. In both the Midwest and Utah, attempts to keep immigrants who had used the fund from defecting may have caused trouble. Some defectors disappeared into neighboring territories and spread bitter tales about the Church. Others who lost their faith but owed nothing to the Church or the community were often allowed to return to the Midwest without argument. The leaders seemed willing to release them, rather than encourage them to stay and stir up trouble among the Saints.

Several Latter-day Saint histories provide information about handcart pioneers, including Howard A. Christy's article, "Handcart Companies," in *Encyclopedia of Mormonism*, Volume 2; Allen and Leonard's *The Story of the Latter-day Saints*; and William Slaughter and Michael Landon's *Trail of Hope: The Story of the Mormon Trail*. I found poignancy and relevance in LeRoy R. Hafen and Ann W. Hafen's *Handcarts to Zion: The Story of a Unique Western Migration 1856–1860*, for it includes journals, accounts, reports, maps, and rosters of all ten handcart companies. The work of Daughter of Utah Pioneers president and historian Kate B. Carter (*Heart Throbs of the West, Our Pioneer Heritage*, and *Treasures of Pioneer History*) provided wonderful anecdotes and details that otherwise would have been lost. Invaluable to me personally and to Saints in general are the excerpts of my Great-great-grand-uncle Reddick N. Allred's diary and its rendering in Rebecca Bartholomew and Leonard Arrington's *Rescue of the 1856 Handcart Companies*.

Seeking non-Mormon perspectives, I was delighted to find one of my favorite writers weighing in: Wallace Stegner's *The Gathering of Zion* and "Ordeal by Handcart" deliver a respectful and honest rendering of the pioneering movement and of the handcart experience. An intelligent discussion of planning errors followed by a heroic but belated rescue by Latter-day Saints can be found in David Roberts's *Devil's Gate: Brigham Young and the Great Mormon Handcart Tragedy*. I had some poignant, if mistaken, insights into these difficulties through family stories about Karen alternately pulling a handcart and herding oxen while crossing the plains.

The genealogical websites Ancestry.com, findagrave.com, and newfamilysearch.org (now defunct) helped me discover new or hidden particulars about my ancestors. The only record more valuable would have been the story provided by the individuals who lived it. Much of what I learned about Karen's passage into Zion came from my father's stories, his autobiography (*The Autobiography of Rulon Clark Allred*), from a few vague stories told by Grandmother Evelyn, and from the hefty book of remembrance commemorating my father's mother's father and his progeny, *The Life of Arthur Benjamin Clark and His Descendants*. I also gained perspective from the biography of Karen's and Mads's son George Henry, *The History of George Rasmussen* by Dora Rasmussen. Some of this material was infused into the biography of Rose and George Rasmussen compiled by Kenneth Rasmussen.

During the second round of revisions, as I searched for more details about Karen and her journey, I visited FamilySearch.org and discovered new postings on Great-great-grandmother Karen's site, particularly *A History of Mads Peter Rasmussen*. The brief biography composed by three daughters of his second and third wives challenged my understanding of those ancestors and some basic assumptions about my entire paternal family. At first I had believed, based on the Arthur B. Clark biography, that Mads was merely a sailor. But in relaying the stories their father told them, Mads's daughters assert that he was first mate on the *Tapscott*. Whether this refers to the 1857 voyage when he first converted to the Church or the 1859 voyage when he emigrated and married Karen, with his seafaring experience, Mads probably made himself very useful to the *William Tapscott*'s crew.

The Rasmussen daughters also say that Mads descended from Danish nobility and that he "was a man of some means." They corroborate the Clark story that he had run away to dodge his obligatory two years in the Danish army. They insist that Mads purchased a wagon and a team of oxen and that he and his new wife had crossed the Great Plains and the Rocky Mountains in relative comfort. As the impression of my handcart grandmother faded away, a new Karen began to take shape, with both stark and shining aspects to her authenticity. A strong-willed woman who braved the consequences of her decisions gradually replaced the long-suffering, endure-to-the-end saint.

Brigham Young's placement of the Rasmussens in Centerville was probably based on the aftermath of the Utah War. Details about this bloodless conflict came from Leonard Arrington's *Brigham Young: American Moses* and Norman F. Furniss's *The Mormon Conflict: 1850–1859*. Some salient information about my ancestors' participation in this and other military clashes — including the practice of having young boys dash before the fire to give the impression that great numbers comprised the Nauvoo Legion — came from my great-grandfather, in *The Life and Times of Byron Harvey Allred, Sr.*, compiled by Byron D. Stout.

The persecution of the Latter-day Saints is recorded in most histories of The Church of Jesus Christ of Latter-day Saints, but the words of Great-great-grandfather William etched in careful script on yellowing copy paper made those onslaughts real for me. Years ago, I struggled to read a photocopy of William's elegant hand, and I am grateful to his great-granddaughter Janice Young for the typed compilation of the *Biography and Journal of William Moore Allred*; revealing that teenaged William was part of the Mormon Militia, that he pursued the Missouri mobs who had burned and looted Mormon properties and raped Latter-day Saint women, and that he was with the militia at Far West, stripped of his weapons and helplessly watching as Missourians called for Joseph Smith's immediate execution. Through William's autobiography and journals, I shared his frustration when he fruitlessly drove his oxen forward while trying to outrace a latecomer with high-stepping horses in his great desire to set the first cornerstone of the Nauvoo Temple. I felt his conflicted presence when the *Nauvoo Expositor* press was burned down and his anxiety when Joseph Smith turned himself in to answer arson charges at Carthage, Illinois. And I felt his deep sorrow when the Prophet's and Hyrum's bodies arrived in Nauvoo, the loss exacerbated by the rage in his heart, a young man's desire to take up his rifle and seek revenge.

The essay about my great-grandmother, Mary Catrena Rasmussen Clark, in *The Life of Arthur Benjamin Clark and His Descendants*, reveals her mother Karen's struggle to adapt to the American West. Some of the harsher details of Karen's life, such as her exile from her parents' home when she converted to the Church, her refusal to speak Danish in her Utah home, and the trouble with Mads that culminated in divorce while she was carrying twins, are described by my father's half-sister, Rhea A. Kunz, in *Voices of Women: Approbating Celestial or Plural Marriage, Volume Two: Treasured Memories*, which is more family history than the apologist treatise on plural marriage the title suggests. But in my family, the two elements, family history and plural marriage, are inseparable.

That Karen learned about the actual practice of the Principle of Plural Marriage in small increments is corroborated by several histories, including Samuel Taylor's *The Kingdom or Nothing*, which describes the influence of plural marriage from its secretive beginnings to the public announcement made by Church Historian Orson Pratt at the 1852 Church Conference held in Salt Lake City.

I wanted to see Karen in the context of other Latter-day Saint women of her time and read extensively about those *grandes dames*.

What I learned could become a book in itself, so I focused on Eliza R. Snow, the woman who replaced Joseph's wife Emma, as Mormondom's first lady after the Prophet's death because she and Karen could have crossed paths. Much has been written about Eliza, who seems to have led a nearly spotless life. Relief Society lesson books provided meaningful accounts of the formation and development of the Relief Society and a well-defined context for Eliza's contributions to that organization and to the Church as a whole. Snow's "Sketch of My Life," contained in Maureen Ursenbach Beecher's compilation *The Personal Writings of Eliza Roxcy Snow*, reveals Eliza's literary talent and her ethereal, bemused approach to life. Todd Compton, author of *In Sacred Loneliness: The Plural Wives of Joseph Smith*, reveals nuances in the relationship between Joseph's first wife, Emma Smith, and his plural wives, giving dimension to the difficulties posed by the Principle of Plural Marriage, and judiciously examines sources, weighing rumors and exhausting archives. Newell and Avery's *Mormon Enigma: Emma Hale Smith, Prophet's Wife, "Elect Lady," Polygamy's Foe* vividly depicts Emma's aversion to polygamy while revealing her salutary character. What emerges from these portraits is a duet of powerful personalities, two women who might have been friends if it hadn't been for polygamy.

Peggy Fletcher Stack's 2016 *Salt Lake Tribune* article, "Shocking Historical Finding: Mormon icon Eliza R. Snow was gang-raped by Missouri ruffians," draws on the research of historian Andrea Radke-Moss into the autobiographical writings of Alice Merrill Horne (daughter of Relief Society President Bathsheba Smith and founder of the first state arts program). Her work in a chapter of an edited book, *Mormon Women's History*, titled "Silent Memories of Missouri: Mormon Women and Men and Sexual Assault in Group Memory and Religious Identity" sheds much-needed light on the puzzle of Eliza's childless state and the tendency to blame it on Joseph's first wife, Emma. It also reveals the co-opting of women's suffering by patriarchal forces intent on bolstering the Church.

Many have written about Joseph Smith's life and his relationship with women. In addition to various Church histories already listed, I found that Donna Hill's *Joseph Smith* and Fawn Brodie's *No Man Knows My History* helped to ground my view in a broader world. Joseph Smith's supportive attitude toward women and his seal of priesthood approval on the Relief Society is described in Beecher and Anderson's *Sisters in Spirit*, particularly in Carol Cornwall Anderson's essay "Mormon Women and the Temple: Toward a New Understanding."

I discovered that a dubious account of John C. Bennett's relationship with Joseph Smith and Mormonism can be glimpsed by plowing through the egregiously slanted *History of the Saints; or, an Expose of Joe Smith and Mormonism*. But a more balanced rendering of Bennett's Mormon adventures comes from Andrew F. Smith's *The Saintly Scoundrel: The Life and Times of Dr. John Cook Bennett*, which also details Bennett's worthy accomplishments, such as establishing medical colleges, serving as company commander for the Union during the Civil War, and pioneering chloroform as anesthesia, contributions that were overshadowed by his unsavory exploitation of the Mormon people.

Writers and publishers who engaged in anti-Mormon polemic inflamed communities against Joseph Smith in particular and Latter-day Saints in general. These range from Alexander Campbell's 1831 article in the *Millennial Harbinger* pamphlet which became the 1832 pamphlet *Delusions* and Eber D. Howe's 1834 collection of affidavits from apostates, *Mormonism Unvailed* [*sic*]. Many derivative pamphlets drew on the two primary works published in the 1830s, inciting Governor Lilburn W. Boggs's Extermination Order in 1838. In 1841, while the Saints were settling in Nauvoo, Thomas Sharp's newspaper, the *Warsaw Signal*, published William Harris's *Mormonism Portrayed*, and continued to fan the flames of persecution by calling for the extermination of Saints in Illinois. After their forced emigration from Missouri, the Saints suffered the consequences of several particularly inflammatory publications in 1842 such as Joshua V. Himes's *Mormon Delusions and Monstrosities*, Reverend John A. Clark's *Gleanings by the Way*, and Jonathan B. Turner's *Mormonism in All Ages*. Two of the most egregious works were a set of anti-Mormon writings by the Reverend Henry Caswall: in 1842, *The City of the Mormons; or, Three Days at Nauvoo* and in 1843, *The Prophet of the Nineteenth Century*.

The *Nauvoo Expositor*, of 1844, featured a single edition edited by Sylvester Emmons and written mainly by excommunicated Latter-day Saints; the destruction of the press led to Joseph Smith's incarceration and death in a Carthage, Illinois, jail cell. These incendiary views were not adequately balanced at the time; few journalists brought a fair perspective to the Latter-day Saint situation. Even today, the heartache and isolation of those persecuted days cannot be fully rendered, although the deeply compassionate *American Crucifixion: The Murder of Joseph Smith and the Fate of the Mormon Church* by Alex Beam attempts to do so.

Concerning the persecutions and the controversies, the library of essays at FairMormon.org has been useful, lending perspectives in the present that help to counter the slanted outpourings of the past. Among these are valuable essays on Joseph Smith and polygamy, on the possibility that children were born of his plural marriages, and regarding the percentage of members who actually practiced polygamy.

Certain florid novels produced after 1852 during the openly polygamous epoch in Utah cast further lurid light on the Latter-day Saints. Women writers penned many of the pattern-setting novels responsible for turning the general public against the people of The Church of Jesus Christ. Some depicted Latter-day Saint patriarchs as depraved criminals who penned up exploited female creatures in harems, as in Ovilla S. Belisle's 1855 book, *The Prophets; or, Mormonism Unveiled*. But Metta Victoria Fuller Victor threw women into the hellish vat, depicting the latter as strumpets in her 1856 *Mormon Wives*.

Despite the vitriol expressed about Saints' attitudes toward sex and gender, Joseph Smith voiced his commitment to help women establish an organization for the sake of their own development and for the good of the community, as revealed in many of the works already cited. His liberal attitude toward women and his willingness to discuss the feminine divine is revealed in various works concerning Joseph Smith and women, including Linda P. Wilcox's essay in *Sisters in Spirit*, "The Mormon Concept of a Mother in Heaven," which takes a penetrating look into Mormon feminism from the earliest days of the Church.

Several histories consider the forces mounting to eradicate polygamy. Shared adversity unified Latter-day Saint men and women in an attempt to preserve the Principle of Plural Marriage; this unity ushered in an extraordinary era for women's growth. *Women of Covenant* does an excellent job of showing that Brigham Young, after his struggle to preempt Emma Smith's influence, relaxed his firm control and expressed a strong appreciation for the sisters' "immense amount of talent." *Women of Covenant* draws from Eliza Roxcy Snow's *Sketch of My Life* and her *Diaries, 1845–1849* to show the respectful dynamic between Mormondom's new first lady and the second President of the Church, Brigham Young, delineating his wish that women receive education and enhancement to preserve their families, to run their homes properly, and to fulfill their lives.

The derogatory words of some polygamous patriarchs toward women, particularly those resistant to polygamy, are contained in announcements and sermons given during the Church's pioneer epoch. *Journal of Discourses, Twenty-Six Volumes* contains certain statements that, when taken out of context, can be seen as misogynist. But Brigham Young and his brethren were under enormous pressure to keep the Latter-day Saints unified and alive; unkind words were countered by many uplifting messages and actions toward and about women. As writers Derr, Cannon, and Beecher show, Brigham Young's clipped attitude toward problematic women extended to problematic men as well and was most obvious during the Utah War, when his martial mindset surfaced everywhere. Contradictions are evident: Brigham Young and other patriarchs opened many doors for Utah women. They were also influenced by millennia of patriarchal structures erected in the "dominator model" as defined by Riane Eisler in *The Chalice and the Blade.* We can only hope that such attitudes are shifting.

The difficulties and rewards for Latter-day Saint women living in polygamy can be found in diaries and journals, although situations are rendered cryptically, and families have been slow to relinquish them. Again, Compton's research offers invaluable, balanced perspectives to counter that of Webb Dee Young Denning, Brigham Young's rebellious plural wife, who inflates and embellishes practices within the polygamous culture in the exposé generally known as *Wife No. Nineteen.*

I know, from observing my father's seven wives, about the heartache associated with living the Principle. I also know that the difficulty of living polygamy has been cached in various diaries and journals of long-suffering Latter-day Saint mothers and grandmothers and great-grandmothers. The frustration and suppression of Latter-day Saint women living polygamy in the early days has been revealed piecemeal and with great reluctance. In some instances, secrecy was necessary in order to protect family members from legal intervention. Such was the case in the journals of Martha Hughes Cannon, and in the journals of my father's wives, who hid their writing to keep it from being used against their husbands and themselves in court. Withholding, whether to protect family or to protect feelings, has shrouded the huge contribution made by plural wives during Utah's polygamous epoch. However, the community-building activities of Utah women are carefully enumerated in books and essays written by women historians, many of them of Latter-day Saint extraction.

The political influence of Latter-day Saint women is carefully and insightfully tracked by Lola Van Wagenen in her *Dialogue: A Journal of Mormon Thought* essay "In Their Own Behalf: The Politicization of Mormon Women and the 1870 Franchise." Beginning with the first organized political venture, a petition that Latter-day Saint women delivered to the governor of Illinois requesting protection for the citizens of Nauvoo, Van Wagenen explores how the women's rights movement and the practice of plural marriage influenced Utah women to become the first female group to vote in a United States general election.

Researching and writing *The Sisterhood: Inside the Lives of Mormon Women* prompted me to identify some of the freedoms Latter-day Saint women gained by pioneering in a polygamous context. Another strong resource for this information written by historian Lawrence Foster, "From Frontier Activism to Neo-Victorian Domesticity: Mormon Women in the Nineteenth and Twentieth Centuries," reveals in broad strokes the changes in the status of women in the Church from one century to the next. Foster's research traces group movements, while the aforementioned Latter-day Saint women's histories map individual gains and contributions of Latter-day Saint women to the sisterhood and to the community. The essay by Grethe Ballif Peterson, "University of Deseret," included in *Encyclopedia of Mormonism*, provides information about the opportunities Brigham Young offered both men and women Latter-day Saints only two-and-a-half years after their arrival in the Salt Lake Valley. Several essays in *Sisters in Spirit*, especially "Gifts of the Spirit: A Woman's Share" by Linda King Newell and Jill Mulvay Derr's "Strength in Our Union: The Making of Mormon Sisterhood," reinforce the immense influence of Latter-day Saint women as they were building Zion. From the same collection, "Precedents for Mormon Women from Scriptures," by Melodie Moench, offers insight into the social incentives of plural marriage, including Brigham Young's conviction that men and women should wholeheartedly invest themselves in raising families, drawing on the parable of the talents to demonstrate the Principle.

In the 1880s, the governmental threats to Latter-day Saint patriarchs intensified, as recounted in various histories, including my go-to resources. The impact of these threats and the encouragement to move into Wyoming Territory, where laws were not so restrictive, was directly experienced by my great-grandfathers as recorded in *The Life of Arthur Benjamin Clark and His Descendants* and *The Life and Times of Byron Harvey Allred, Sr.* and by my grandfather, Byron Harvey Allred, Jr., in *History of the Life and Acts of Byron Harvey Allred, Jr.*

The online apologist piece, "Polygamy: The Mormon Enigma," helped me understand the progression of US legislative forays launched to eradicate polygamy, the mounting of Pinkertons and U.S. Marshals to arrest polygamous patriarchs, and the Church's response to federal interference. Reading about the subterfuge of earlier days stirred memories of my childhood terror, such as hiding in the basement and praying that the police would not search the house and find me, proof that my father had not kept the promise given to the parole board, that he would not practice polygamy.

As a young woman, I knew nothing of the enfranchisement of Utah women, twenty-six of whom cast their votes in the first general election. I was not taught about it in state history classes or in Church. When my blood ran hot because a male social studies teacher told me I didn't know what I was talking about, when my big brother laughed at my attempts to articulate women's rights, I didn't know where to turn for an example that would assuage and redirect my feelings. If I had known that I could turn to the Relief Society Minutes housed in Church offices to read about the circumstances, events, and speeches surrounding the "Great Indignation Meeting of 1870," I would have summoned self-respect; I wouldn't have been so strident and reckless in acting out my anger as a teenager. In her book, *Pedestals & Podiums*, Martha Sonntag Bradley describes the impact of this gathering on the character and self-perception of early Latter-day Saint women and reveals the stark contrast of these pioneer paragons to modern women in the Church who surrendered most of their personal power to right-wing politics during the 1970s and 1980s. Bradley's work suggests that idealization of the past can thwart our present experience and warp our expectations of the future. She concludes that both sets of women primarily intended to fulfill the wishes of Church leaders rather than acting in the best interests of themselves, their children, and other women.

For wider perspective on ways the national women's movement framed Latter-day Saint women's attempts to validate their polygamous way of life, I turned to Ellen Carol DuBois, *Feminism and Suffrage*, and Eleanor Flexner, *Century of Struggle*. These books explore the influence of the National Woman Suffrage Association on Utah women's franchise, the complexities of Church agendas, and how the polygamy issue deepened the crevasse between prominent women's groups. These volumes show how Utah women swelled the ranks of the NWSA and influenced future agendas, citing ways Latter-day Saint women promoted national and international women's rights.

The story of building the railroad in Weber Canyon has been effectively rendered in *A History of Morgan County*, by Linda Smith, who reveals the preliminary work building trestles across a harrowing landscape. The tale of how the golden spike joined the Central and Pacific Railroads at Promontory Summit, Utah, to form the Transcontinental Railway and facilitate cross-country travel was also well told in a *Utah History Encyclopedia* entry by Deborah Blake. The Golden Spike event is celebrated yearly in Ogden, Utah, with a spike-driving reenactment.

I found information about Karen's and Mads's experience crossing the plains, and details about Mads's parents and siblings, in the previously mentioned *A History of Mads Peter Rasmussen*. This biography really turned the lights on for me, yielding important details about my great-great-grandparents' marriage, economic status, divorce, and subsequent years. For information about Karen's parents and the siblings who emigrated to Utah after Karen and Mads had settled in Richville, I turned to the *History of Ane Margrethe Baltzarsdatter*, compiled by Chandelle Hill Brough and posted by Clayton Brough on FamilySearch.org. Additional details were gleaned from *A Biography of Mary Catrena Rasmussen (1864–1938)* compiled from family records by another great-granddaughter, Janeen Christensen, and posted on FamilySearch.org. Her account, combining oral and written histories, corroborates details I learned from my immediate family histories, journals, and autobiographies as well as conversations with my father, my aunt Rhea Kunz, and other family members. The family photos in the Allred Family Album collected by my youngest sister, Mary Dawn Allred, have illustrated the family saga provided by various accounts. There is a photo of Mary Catrena and the white dress she made for her little sister to wear to their grandmother's funeral and of the Richville house made of railroad ties. For these and all other resources, I am enormously grateful.

For me, Great-great-grandmother Karen is an iteration of human possibility. If I can play devil's advocate for a moment, the Gospel or any religion could be the opiate Karl Marx abhorred, a way of making people into "sheeple" fleeced by someone else's agenda. I could spend my life practicing for eternity and the institution could betray me. Yet, I crave paradise, the experience of joy and communion. What else can I do than be accountable for my experience, offering my belief as it registers in my being? Holding fast to my birthright and agency, I know that it's up to me. If the spiritual inheritance bestowed by my ancestors dies, it is dead in me; if it lives, it lives in me. It's always my choice. I create the context.

I think of Karen's brave stand to embrace a new life, and I'm reminded of my earliest understandings of choices declared and enacted. It is spring. The white-shirted fundamentalist teacher glowers down at three-and-a-half-year-old me as I wriggle and giggle with the sap of life, and he pronounces, "Jesus doesn't like it when you do that." I look up at him and smile. "Yes, he does. He likes it." Words are crucial in sculpting life. Consider the powerful verse, John 1:1. "In the beginning was the Word, and the Word was with God, and the Word was God," which reminds us that as children of God, we can speak anything into being. With our voices, we can generate hell in a heartbeat. Instead of war and sorrow, we can wield peace and love. First one must own one's voice; one must insist on speaking truly and being heard. Those brave souls who honestly relate their part in the human cavalcade, as did the people who created these invaluable bibliographic sources, are simultaneously healing previous generations and engendering those yet to come. By exercising agency and accountability, we members of the human family can transcend dark history and prompt our children and grandchildren to live more authentic and fulfilling lives. Together we can create wide fields of heaven on Earth.

Bibliography & Further Reading

Abarca, Meredith. *Voices in the Kitchen.* College Station, TX: Texas A&M University Press, 2006.

Allen, James B. and Glen M. Leonard. *The Story of the Latter-day Saints.* Salt Lake City: Deseret Book Company, 1976.

Allred Family Newsletter. Official publication of the Allred Family Organization, Inc. www.Allredfamily.org.

Allred, Byron Harvey, Jr. *History of the Life and Acts of Byron Harvey Allred, Jr.* Compiled by Owen Arthur Allred. Allred Family archives.

Allred, Byron Harvey, Sr. *The Life and Times of Byron Harvey Allred, Sr.* [Based on his personal diaries.] Compiled by Byron D. Stout, 1997. Allred Family archives.

Allred, Mabel Finlayson. *Plural Wife: The Life Story of Mabel Finlayson Allred.* Edited by Martha Bradley-Evans. Logan, UT: Utah State University Press, 2012.

Allred, Reddick N. *The Diary of Reddick N. Allred.* Salt Lake City: Daughters of Utah Pioneers collection, 1828–1963.

Allred, Rulon Clark. *The Allred Family in America.* Salt Lake City: The Allred Family Organization, Volume 1, 1969.

———. *The Autobiography of Rulon Clark Allred.* Ancestry.com.

———. *Journals, 1929–1977.* Allred Family archives.

———. *A Short History of Isaac Allred.* Allred Family archives.

———. *The Story of My Life in Brief.* Allred Family archives.

Allred, William Moore. *Biography and Journal of William Moore Allred.* Compiled by Janice Young. Allred Family archives.

Anderson, Carol Cornwall. "Mormon Women and the Temple:

Toward a New Understanding." In *Sisters in Spirit: Mormon Women in Historical and Cultural Perspective*, edited by Maureen Ursenbach Beecher and Lavina Fielding Anderson. Chicago: University of Illinois Press, 1987.

Arrington, Leonard J. *Brigham Young: American Moses*. New York: Alfred A. Knopf, 1985.

Arrington, Leonard J. and David Bitton. *The Mormon Experience: A History of the Latter-day Saints*. New York: Alfred A. Knopf, 1979.

Bartholomew, Rebecca and Leonard J. Arrington. *Rescue of the 1856 Handcart Companies*. Salt Lake City: Signature Books, 1993.

Beam, Alex. *American Crucifixion: The Murder of Joseph Smith and the Fate of the Mormon Church*. New York: Public Affairs, Perseus Book Group, 2014.

Beecher, Maureen Ursenbach and Lavina Fielding Anderson, eds. *Sisters in Spirit: Mormon Women in Historical and Cultural Perspective*. Chicago: University of Illinois Press, 1987.

Belisle, Ovilla S. *The Prophets; or, Mormonism Unveiled*. London: Charles H. Clarke, 1855.

Bennett, John C. *History of the Saints; or, an Expose of Joe Smith and Mormonism*. Boston, MA: Leland & Whiting, 1842.

Blake, Deborah. "Golden Spike National Historic Site." *Utah History Encyclopedia*. Salt Lake City: University of Utah Press, 1994.

Bradley, Martha Sonntag. *Pedestals & Podiums: Utah Women, Religious Authority and Equal Rights*. Salt Lake City: Signature Books, 2005.

Brodie, Fawn. *No Man Knows My History*. New York: Alfred Knopf, 1945.

Bushman, Richard Lyman. *Mormonism: A Very Short Introduction*. New York: Oxford University Press, 2008.

Carter, Kate B. *Heart Throbs of the West*. Salt Lake City: Daughters of the Utah Pioneers, 1940.

———. *Our Pioneer Heritage*. Salt Lake City: Daughters of the Utah Pioneers, 1958.

———. *Treasures of Pioneer History*. Salt Lake City: Daughters of the Utah Pioneers, 1959.

Campbell, Alexander. "Delusions." *Millennial Harbinger*, 1832 pamphlet *Delusions*, included in Eber D. Howe's 1834 collection of affidavits from apostates, *Mormonism Unvailed* [sic].

Caswall, Reverend Henry. *The City of the Mormons or Three Days at Nauvoo.* London: J. G. F. and J. Rivington, 1842.

——. *The Prophet of the Nineteenth Century, or The Rise, Progress and Present State of the Mormons or Latter-day Saints.* London: J. G. F. and J. Rivington, 1843.

Christy, Howard A. "Handcart Companies." In *Encyclopedia of Mormonism*, edited by Daniel Ludlow. New York: Macmillan, 1992.

Church of Jesus Christ of Latter-day Saints History Library, https://history.churchofjesuschrist.org.

Clark, Reverend John A. *Gleanings by the Way.* New York: W. J. & J. K. Simon, 1842.

Compton, Todd. *In Sacred Loneliness: The Plural Wives of Joseph Smith.* Salt Lake City: Signature Books, 1997.

Cook, Verla Clark, ed. *The Life of Arthur Benjamin Clark and His Descendants, Book of Remembrance.* Salt Lake City: Utah State Historical Society, 1971.

Danish Society for Emigration History (in collaboration with Danes Worldwide Archives). https://danishamericanarchive.com.

Daughters in My Kingdom: The History and Work of Relief Society. Corporation of the President of The Church of Jesus Christ of Latter-day Saints, Salt Lake City: LDS Church, 2010.

Denning, Ann Eliza Webb Dee Young. *Wife No. Nineteen.* Reprinted with revisions as *Nineteenth Wife, Being a Complete Expose of Mormonism, and Revealing the Sorrows, Sacrifices and Sufferings of Women in Polygamy.* Hartford, CT: Dustin, Gilman & Co., 1875.

Derr, Jill Mulvay. "Strength in Our Union: The Making of Mormon Sisterhood." In *Sisters in Spirit: Mormon Women in Historical and Cultural Perspective*, edited by Maureen Ursenbach Beecher and Lavina Fielding Anderson. Chicago: University of Illinois Press, 1987.

Derr, Jill Mulvay, Janath Russell Cannon, and Maureen Ursenbach Beecher. *Women of Covenant: The Story of Relief Society.* Salt Lake City: Deseret Book Company and Provo: Brigham Young University Press, 1992.

DuBois, Ellen Carol. *Feminism and Suffrage: The Emergence of an Independent Women's Movement in America, 1848–1869.* Ithaca, NY: Cornell University Press, 1978.

Eisler, Riane. *The Chalice and the Blade.* San Francisco, CA: Harper and Row, 1987.

FairMormon.org. (Formerly Foundation for Apologetic Information & Research.)

The Family: A Proclamation to the World. The First Presidency and Twelve Apostles of the Church of Jesus Christ of Latter-day Saints, September 23, 1995. https://www.lds.org/topics/family-proclamation.

FamilySearch.org: *Autobiography of Lucius Clark (1886–1981)*; *A Biography of Mary Catrena Rasmussen (1864–1938)* [compiled by Janeen Christensen]; *History of Ane Margrethe Baltzarsdatter* [compiled by Chandelle Hill Brough]; *The History of George Rasmussen* [compiled by Dora Rasmussen]; *History of Mads Peter Rasmussen.*

Flexner, Eleanor. *Century of Struggle: The Woman's Rights Movement in the United States.* Cambridge, MA: Harvard University Press, 1959.

Foster, Lawrence. "From Frontier Activism to Neo-Victorian Domesticity: Mormon Women in the Nineteenth and Twentieth Centuries." *Journal of Mormon History*, Vol. 6 (1979): 3–21.

Furniss, Norman F. *The Mormon Conflict: 1850–1859.* New Haven, CT: Yale University Press, 1960.

Hafen, LeRoy R. and Ann W. Hafen. *Handcarts to Zion: The Story of a Unique Western Migration 1856–1860.* London: Arthur H. Clark Company, 1960 and Lincoln: University of Nebraska Press, 1981.

Harris, William. *Mormonism Portrayed.* Newberry Library Collection. Warsaw, IL: Sharp & Gamble, 1841.

Hill, Donna. *Joseph Smith.* Garden City, NY: Doubleday & Company, 1977.

Himes, Joshua V., ed. *Mormon Delusions and Monstrosities.* Boston: Joshua V. Himes, 1842.

Hobbs, Henry. "The Journal of Henry Hobbs, 1835–1917." In *William Tapscott: Liverpool to New York/Mormon Migration.* Provo, UT: Harold B. Lee Library, Brigham Young University, 2011.

Horsbrugh-Porter, Anna. *Created Equal: Voices on Women's Rights.* New York: Palgrave Macmillan, 2009.

Howick, E. Keith. "Polygamy: The Mormon Enigma: Historical Overview." WindRiver Publishing, Inc., 2007. http://www.polygamy-faq.com/history.php.

Hwang, Deok-Sang, Sun Kwang Kim, and Hyunsu Bae.

"Therapeutic Effects of Bee Venom on Immunological and Neurological Diseases." Toxins (Basel), July 29, 2015, 7(7): 2413–2421, https://www.ncbi.nlm.nih.gov/pmc/articles/PMC4516920/.

Jenson, Andrew. *History of the Scandinavian Mission*. Salt Lake City: Deseret News Press, 1927.

Jones, Carrie Mouritsen and Jerald Olean Seelos. *The Mourits Mouritsen Family: A Record of His Posterity and His Ancestors*. FamilySearch.org, January 1982.

Kristof, Nicholas D. and Sheryl WuDunn. *Half the Sky: Turning Oppression into Opportunity for Women Worldwide*. New York: Random House, 2009.

Kunz, Rhea Allred. *Voices of Women: Approbating Celestial or Plural Marriage*, Volumes I and II. Draper, UT: Review and Purview Publishers, 1985.

Lubbock, Basil. *The Western Ocean Packets*. West Haven, NY: J. Brown & Son, 1925; Mineola, NY: Dover Publications, 1988.

Ludlow, Daniel H., ed. *Encyclopedia of Mormonism*. New York: Macmillan, 1992.

Matteson, Edith and Jean Matteson. "Mormon Influence on Scandinavian Settlement in Nebraska." In *On Distant Shores: Proceedings of the Marcus Lee Hansen Immigration Conference*: Aalborg, Denmark, June 29–July 1, 1992. Danish Society for Emigration History in collaboration with Danes Worldwide Archives. http://www.xmission.com/~nelsonb/nebraska.htm.

Moench, Melodie. "Precedents for Mormon Women from Scriptures." In *Sisters in Spirit: Mormon Women in Historical and Cultural Perspective*, edited by Maureen Ursenbach Beecher and Lavina Fielding Anderson. Chicago: University of Illinois Press, 1987.

Mormon Migration Database. Brigham Young University Library online: http://lib.byu.edu

Mormon Overland Travel Database. Church History Library online. https://history.churchofjesuschrist.org.

Mulder, William. *Homeward to Zion: The Mormon Migration from Scandinavia*. Minneapolis: University of Minnesota Press, 1957.

———. *The Mormons in American History*. Salt Lake City: University of Utah Press, 1981.

Nauvoo Expositor. Sylvester Emmons, editor and writer. Nauvoo, Illinois, 1844.

Neslen, Robert. "Letter to Asa Calkin." *Millennial Star* 21:25, June

18, 1859.

Newell, Linda King. "Gifts of the Spirit: A Woman's Share." In *Sisters in Spirit: Mormon Women in Historical and Cultural Perspective*, edited by Maureen Ursenbach Beecher and Lavina Fielding Anderson. Chicago: University of Illinois Press, 1987.

Newell, Linda King and Valeen Tippetts Avery. *Mormon Enigma: Emma Hale Smith, Prophet's Wife, Elect Lady, Polygamy's Foe*. Garden City, NY: Doubleday, 1984.

Peterson, Grethe Ballif. "University of Deseret." *Encyclopedia of Mormonism*. New York: Macmillan, 1992.

Radke-Moss, Andrea. "Silent Memories of Missouri: Mormon Women and Men and Sexual Assault in Group Memory and Religious Identity." In *Mormon Women's History: Beyond Biography*, edited by Rachel Cope, Amy Easton-Flake, Keith Erekson, and Lisa Olsen Tait. Vancouver, BC: Fairleigh Dickinson University Press, 2017.

Roberts, David. *Devil's Gate: Brigham Young and the Great Mormon Handcart Tragedy*. New York: Simon and Schuster, 2008.

Rothenberg, Paula S., ed. *Race, Class, and Gender in the United States*. New York: Worth Publishers, 2010.

Saints by Sea: Latter-day Saint Immigration to America. saintsbysea. lib.byu.edu.

Seljaas, Helge. "Polygamy among the Norwegian Saints." *Norwegian-American Studies*, Vol. 27, 2000. Norwegian-American Historical Association (NAHA). https://www.naha.stolaf.edu.

Shipps, Jan. *Mormonism: The Story of a New Religious Tradition*. Chicago: University of Illinois Press, 1992.

Slaughter, William and Michael Landon. *Trail of Hope: The Story of the Mormon Trail*. Salt Lake City: Deseret Book, 1997.

Smith, Andrew F. *The Saintly Scoundrel: The Life and Times of Dr. John Cook Bennett*. Urbana and Chicago, IL: University of Illinois Press, 1997.

Smith, Ellen Johanna Larson. *The Life of Mons Larson (1823–1890)*. www/ancestorpages.com/fr_mons.html.

Smith, Joseph. "Church History." *The Joseph Smith Papers*. Salt Lake City: Church Historian's Press.

———. *Journal of Discourses*, Volumes 1–26. [Compilation of services and other materials.]

———. "Times and Seasons." *The Joseph Smith Papers*. Salt Lake City:

Church Historian's Press.

Smith, Linda. *A History of Morgan County*. Utah Centennial History Series. Salt Lake City: Utah State Historical Society, Morgan County Commission, 1999.

Snow, Eliza R. "Sketch of My Life." In *The Personal Writings of Eliza Roxcy Snow*, edited by Maureen Ursenbach Beecher. Logan, UT: Utah State University Press, 2000.

Snow, Eliza R. *Diaries, 1845–1849*. Holograph, San Marino, CA: Huntington Library.

Solomon, Dorothy Allred, *Daughter of the Saints*. New York: W. W. Norton, 2004. (First edition published as *Predators, Prey, and Other Kinfolk: Growing up in Polygamy*. New York: W.W. Norton, 2003.)

Solomon, Dorothy Allred. *In My Father's House: A Memoir of Polygamy*. Lubbock, TX: Texas Tech University Press, 2009. (First edition, New York: Franklin Watts, 1984.)

Solomon, Dorothy Allred. *The Sisterhood: Inside the Lives of Mormon Women*. New York: Palgrave Macmillan, 2007.

Sonne, Conway B. *Ships, Saints, and Mariners: A Maritime Encyclopedia of Mormon Migration, 1830–1890*. Salt Lake City: University of Utah Press, 1987.

Sorenson, Kirsten. "Shipwrecked Saints Intrigue Curator: Display of Artifacts Planned, Survivors' Descendants Sought." http://www.xmission/nelsonb/wrecked.htm.

Stack, Peggy Fletcher. "Shocking Historical Finding: Mormon Icon Eliza R. Snow Was Gang-Raped by Missouri Ruffians." *Salt Lake Tribune*, March 3, 2016.

State, Katherine Handy Allred. *Memories of Katherine Handy Allred State*. Allred Family archives.

Stegner, Wallace. *The Gathering of Zion: The Story of the Mormon Trail*. New York: McGraw Hill, 1964/Bison Books, 1992.

———. "Ordeal by Handcart." *Collier's Weekly*, July 6, 1956.

Taylor, Samuel W. *The Kingdom or Nothing: The Life of John Taylor, Militant Mormon*. New York: Macmillan and London: Collier Macmillan Publishers, 1976. Reprinted as *The Last Pioneer: John Taylor, a Mormon Prophet*. Salt Lake City: Signature Books, 1999.

Turner, Jonathan B. *Mormonism in All Ages*. Mountain View, CA: Sagwan Press, Creative Media Partners, 2015. (First publication, New York: Platt and Peters, 1842.)

Van Wagenen, Lola. "In Their Own Behalf: The Politicization of Mormon Women and the 1870 Franchise," *Dialogue: A Journal of Mormon Thought*, vol. 24, no. 4, Winter 1991.

Van Wagoner, Richard S. *Mormon Polygamy: A History.* Salt Lake City: Signature Books, 1989.

Victor, Metta Victoria Fuller. *Mormon Wives: A Narrative of Facts Stranger Than Fiction.* New York: Derby & Jackson, 1856.

White, Jean Bickmore. "Woman's Place is in the Constitution." *Utah State Historical Quarterly*, 42, Fall 1974.

Wilcox, Linda P. "The Mormon Concept of a Mother in Heaven." In *Sisters in Spirit: Mormon Women in Historical and Cultural Perspective*, edited by Maureen Ursenbach Beecher and Lavina Fielding Anderson. Chicago: University of Illinois Press, 1987.

Woolf, Virginia. *A Room of One's Own.* Surrey/London, UK: Hogarth Press, 1929.

Index

Established in recognition of a lifetime of achievement in and dedication to scholarly publishing, Judith Keeling Books honor works undertaken through careful research and assiduous attention to detail that make a valuable, perhaps otherwise unnoticed, contribution to the scholarly community and to the literary culture of Texas and the American West.